Praise for *The Third Choice*:

"*The Third Choice* is the most helpful, complete, loving guide for birth parents that I have read."

—Debbie Parelskin, MSW, co-author, *My Special Family*

"An essential resource for pregnant women considering adoption, it is also recommended to their partners, their families, and prospective adoptive parents who will gain a fuller understanding of the experience of the women whose collaboration is essential to their forming a family."

—Anne C. Bernstein, author of *Flight of the Stork: What Children Think (and When) about Sex and Family Building*

"*Third Choice* is a book I give to every birth mother who consults with me...I could not wait until this revised edition came out to share it again with expectant birth parents and with their adoptive parents."

—Susan Romer, Ph.D., J.D., adoption attorney

"...respect and kindness permeate the book—not only for the adopting family but to the birthmother, birthfather, and child. The book addresses the practical and the emotional..."

—Lynn Mannix, MFTC, executive director, California Counseling Institute

"[Foge and Mosconi] are respectful of the conflicting emotions experienced by women with unplanned pregnancies and are also aware of the myriad decisions that have to be made. They cover a lot of ground...This book is recommended for public libraries."

—*Library Journal*

"...written intelligently and without judgement—an obvious tribute for the right of birth parents to be treated with respect and dignity."

—Michelle Fried, Adoption S.T.A.R.

"…thought-provoking and touching…This book is also a great resource for every therapist to have on his or her shelf."
—*The California Therapist*, the magazine of the California Association of Marriage and Family Therapists (CAMFT)

"…the contents of this book applies to a specialized and often overlooked audience of birth mothers. I particularly enjoyed the updated information on open adoption and the step-by-step guide through the process of adoption."
—Mary Martin Mason, author of *Make Room for Daddy*

"Written with great clarity and compassion, *The Third Choice* is an invaluable resource for pregnant women considering adoption."
—Jana Wolff, author, *Secret Thoughts of an Adoptive Mother*

"…this book cuts through the confusion, frustration, fear, and disappointment surrounding an untimely pregnancy…A must read…"
Lesley Siegel, adoption attorney

"…a very complete book. And answers just about any questions anyone would ask about adoption."
—April Anderson, adoptive birthmother

THE THIRD CHOICE

A Woman's Guide to
Placing a Child for Adoption

SECOND EDITION

Adoption Connection
Call: 1 (800) 972-9225
www.AdoptionConnection.Org
families@AdoptionConnection.Org

THE THIRD CHOICE

A Woman's Guide
to
Placing a Child for Adoption

SECOND EDITION

by

Leslie Foge, M.A., M.F.T.

and

Gail Mosconi, M.S.W., L.C.S.W.

THIRD CHOICE BOOKS
SOLSTICE PRESS
Oakland · 2004

For information contact:
Third Choice Books
www.Thirdchoicebooks.com
6114 La Salle Avenue Box 744
Oakland, California 94611-2802

Printed by Solstice Press
www.solsticepress.com

Cover painting " Madonna and Child"
by Don S. Ellis

0-88739-575-9 Paper
Library of Congress Catalog Number 2003103386
Printed in the United States of America

This book is dedicated to
Sean, Scott, Gina, and Aleah

and to the many birth
and adoptive families who have
allowed us to be a part of their lives.

Table of Contents

Acknowledgements

We wish to thank the many people who contributed their time, energy, ideas, and loving support to help bring this book to print.

First and foremost, we wish to acknowledge Maureen Pierce, without whom this project would never have gotten off the ground. Her enthusiasm and vision were invaluable.

We are eternally grateful for the support and guidance we received from our colleagues at the Independent Adoption Center. It was through our work there, initially, that we gained the knowledge and expertise that prompted us to write this book. Many of the procedures outlined in this book were developed from protocols used at this agency.

We wish to thank Beverly Williscroft, Lesley Siegel, Sarah Jensen, and Cara Helberg for helping us gather comments and quotes from birthmothers. The actual words of birthmothers added authenticity and depth to our manuscript.

Many people graciously offered feedback and editorial suggestions. In particular: Patricia Martinez Dorner for her thorough and thoughtful response to our manuscript; Debbie Parelskin for her undaunting optimism; Beth Hall and Gail Steinberg of PACT for their support; Mary Martin Mason for her sensitive comments about birthfathers. And we are most grateful to Ellen Roseman, of Cooperative Adoption Consulting and Susan Romer, J.D., for their wholehearted belief in our book and their relentless and enthusiastic support.

Finally, we are indebted to our printer, Richard Engle, and the staff at Solstice Press. They were instrumental in bringing this second edition to print and have always been incredibly encouraging and helpful.

Introduction:
AN ADOPTION RENAISSANCE

The Legacy of Closed Adoption

Prior to the 1970s, the practice of adoption consisted primarily of what we now call a "closed" adoption. A woman who considered placing her child for adoption was not allowed to make decisions about who would adopt her child, and she certainly was not allowed to meet the adopting couple or learn information about them which could lead her to find and contact this new family. It was also standard practice that when a baby was to be placed for adoption at birth or shortly thereafter, the birthmother and her family were not allowed to see, touch, hold, or say good-bye to the baby before placement. Some women were not even allowed to know the gender of their child.

In agency adoptions, babies often went directly from the hospital to temporary placement in a foster home while legal issues were resolved, the health of the child was established, and suitable parents were found. As adults, many adoptees are finding out that they actually spent weeks or months in foster care before they were placed with their adoptive parents.

The practice of closed adoption was developed for a variety of reasons, all rooted in the beliefs and morals of the late nineteenth and early twentieth centuries. Closed adoption evolved from a need for privacy to protect the reputation of the birthmother and save her and her family from the shame of an out-of-wedlock birth. During those times, there was little tolerance in society for single parents, unless it was the result of widowhood. The idea of parenting without first being married was unheard of and carried great shame and social isolation. Social workers and those controlling the adoption process

1

also believed that they, as professionals, were better equipped than the birthmother to make decisions about what was best for the child. They did not believe that a woman who had already made one bad decision, namely sex outside of marriage, had the capacity or the right to decide what would be best for her child. They also believed that if a birthmother got too involved with the adoption or with the baby—knowing who the adoptive parents were, seeing the baby, spending time with the child before placement—she would not be able to separate from the baby and the adoption would be too hard on her. Professionals were taught that birthmothers needed to put this chapter of their life behind them and go on as if nothing had ever happened.

Another prevailing belief that supported the practice of closed adoption was that babies were born without a history and could be treated as "blank slates" upon which the new adoptive family would instill their own history, lifestyle, values, and character. This belief helped adoptive parents feel a sense of entitlement to their adopted children and relieved them of any fear that the "bad" character of the birthmother could be passed on to the child. But it also did a tremendous disservice to the child, who did, indeed, come to his or her new family with an abundance of racial, ethnic, genetic, and medical history.

An Open Adoption Renaissance

In the 1970s, the practice of adoption began to undergo a profound change as the needs, desires, and concerns of all members of the adoption triad—birth parents, prospective adoptive parents, and adoptees—began to intersect. At the time, a variety of factors reduced the number of pregnant women choosing adoption: the availability of birth control and abortion; the relaxation of social mores, which allowed single women to parent without as much social disapproval; and increased access to government aid programs to help support women and children. All of these factors meant there were fewer infants available for adoption than in the past.

This reduction in the availability of adoptable infants came at the same time as the number of people wanting to adopt hit an all-time high. The baby-boom generation (those born from 1945 to 1965) began to come of age. They had delayed their own childbearing to go to college and build careers. Now, they were getting married, settling down, and throwing away their birth control—and to their surprise, not getting pregnant. In fact, the baby-boom generation is the first to suffer from near-epidemic proportions of infertility.

A number of factors led to this rise in infertility. Some baby-boomers simply delayed childbearing until their late '30s and early '40s and found that the delay decreased their chances of a successful pregnancy. Other women and men suffered long-term side effects and reproductive damage from using unsafe methods of birth control or from sexually transmitted diseases that caused scarring of the reproductive organs. There were other factors, but these two were the most widespread and had the most significant impact.

The two social problems collided. On the one hand, young women were no longer choosing adoption because they could now get birth control, have a legal abortion, or be a single parent, thus reducing the number of infants available for adoption. On the other hand, there were large numbers of infertile couples wanting to adopt.

Around this same time, a number of people across the country who had been placed for adoption through the traditional closed adoption process were beginning to search for information about their original families. Some of the adoptees were even uncovering the identity of their birthfamilies and setting up reunions. These adult adoptees were reporting that, while many of them had been raised with love and comfort by their adoptive parents, they continued to wonder about their original family, their background, and the reason they had been placed for adoption. They each felt somehow "unfinished" or had an unexplained empty place within themselves caused by not knowing the same basic information non-adoptees take for granted, such as where they came from, what their health background was, and how they came to be in their present family.

Birthparents and adoptees were beginning to speak more publicly about the painful impact that adoption had on their lives. The practice of traditional adoption began to evolve when some progressive adoption professionals started listening and responding to residual pain expressed by adult adoptees and birthparents. These adoption counselors and social workers were hoping to address the many unanswered questions about the children's history, thus promoting better emotional health for adopted children and birthparents.

As these voices began to emerge, a common solution within the adoption community began to take shape. Instead of abolishing adoption or classifying it as an undesirable choice born of desperation, secrecy, and shame, what if we changed it? Made it more open? Made it more humane? What would happen if the process were truly controlled by those involved in the adoption? What if birthmothers were the ones to choose the family their child would be adopted into? What if they could actually meet the new parents? What would happen if a birthmother got to see, hold, and spend time with her baby after the birth before placing the baby with the new parents? Could we imagine an adoption where the birthparents, the adoptive parents, and the child stayed in contact with each other following placement? For how long? Forever?

As these options were made available to young women in the early 1980s, mostly through private or independent adoption (non-agency), it became clear that not only was adoption itself transforming before our very eyes, but that these new elements of openness had powerful (and we believe positive) potential for the future mental and emotional health of adoptees, as well as for adoptive parents and birthfamilies.

"I could never imagine having a complete stranger raise my baby."
"If I chose adoption, I would never know if my child was all right."
"I couldn't stand not ever being able to see or hold my baby."
"What if the adopting parents didn't love my child?"
"The thought of my child going into foster care is just too much."

The change in adoption practice from a closed system to a more open one is not without its detractors and critics, however. Some experts believe openness in adoption can prolong the grieving and letting-go process for birthmothers, keeping them trapped in a state of quasi-parenthood, unable to move on emotionally with their lives. Others believe adoptees will be confused about who their "real" parents are and will never feel quite as well grounded in their adoptive families. Some also fear the adoptive parents will never feel truly entitled to their children with the birthparents or birth relatives still in contact, and think this interferes with family bonding. Still others have expressed concern that since open adoption, which allows the birthmother ongoing contact over a lifetime, is not a legal guarantee, some adoptive parents will use the promise of openness in order to adopt a baby but will not live up to that promise, thus giving birthmothers unrealistic expectations.

Open adoption is not entirely a new concept in this country. Prior to institutional adoptions, which emerged in the late 1800s, adoptions were often handled within the family or community. A young daughter who got pregnant without the benefit of marriage was hidden, the pregnancy disguised under lots of clothing, and sometimes she was sent off to visit a relative, only to return alone some months later, having left the baby to be raised by another family member. Sometimes an older married sister or the girl's own mother would raise the child as her own.

Resourceful and desperate families developed these solutions, and while all the family members knew the truth, the truth was not spoken, and people went on with their lives in their newly assigned roles. That was not the healthiest way to deal with adoption. Often it was a huge family secret, the consequences of which rested most heavily on the shoulders of the adoptee, who was usually the last to know. We do know from this history, however, that birthmothers can relinquish their role as mother, even while remaining in physical contact with the child.

The vast majority of birthmothers we have worked with as adoption counselors say that by participating actively in their adoption plan—choosing and meeting the new parents; seeing, holding, and spending time with their baby before placement; and establishing ongoing contact with the adopting family—they are able to have greater ownership over their choice. They feel more confident, grieve their loss more concretely, feel more complete about their decision, and have a greater sense of pride, accomplishment, and peace of mind knowing they did their best.

For Children

Since the recent history of open adoption has been brief, the adoption community is just beginning to conduct research on the outcome of open adoption for children, and the results are positive. This is where the ultimate test of the success of openness will be found. It is wonderful that birthmothers and adoptive families feel they have benefited from openness, but one cannot automatically assume openness is best for the children.

Any child who is separated from his or her birthparent, the mother in particular, will experience the wound of that very primal loss. This is true whether the loss occurs through adoption, divorce, death, illness, or other circumstances. However, in their book, _Children of Open Adoption,_ Kathleen Silber and Patricia Dorner report that children from open adoptions are usually well adjusted, happy, and clear on their relationships with the adoptive parents and birthparents. In fact, they say the most common response from kids discussing their adoption is "What's the big deal?"

Of course, adoption is a big deal for birthparents, adoptive parents, and children, and we don't want to minimize its importance in shaping the lives of all who live it. Open adoption does not solve all of the problems that have been associated with closed adoption. Sometimes, open adoption itself can bring challenges and complexities not experienced with closed adoption. However, it can also offer the birthparents some peace of mind, the adoptive parents valuable information about the child they will be accepting into their family, and the adoptee a sense of rootedness, history, and, ultimately, belonging.

The Birthparent Experience

Birthmothers are speaking out more and more about how profoundly their adoption experience has affected their lives. Personal memoirs are being written and published by birthmothers as a way of giving voice to their years of emotional suffering. The internet is replete with websites of birthmoms who are reaching out to connect with other women who know their struggles on a visceral level. Birthmother support groups and reunion search groups are forming across the country as birthmoms are coming forth to tell their stories and receive validation. In birthmother circles, there is exploration about how the act of placing a child for adoption has reverberated through their lives and intertwined with their emotional, psychological, social and behavioral struggles. One birthmother on the web says,

"...emotional numbness gives way to pain in the form of depression, anger, self-esteem and shame."

Our observations as adoption counselors are that at least a portion of the lifelong process of adoption loss and pain can be traced back to circumstances around which the adoption itself was conducted. As long as birthparents are not fully involved in the adoption process, and not truly valued and respected, there is the risk of shame and self-doubt.

On the other hand, we have witnessed firsthand birthmothers who, while acknowledging ongoing grief, also see themselves involved in an adoption characterized by mutual love and integrity.

Our hopes in writing this book, and subsequently this second edition, is that by creating humane, healthy, and compassionate adoptions, birthmothers will have a greater chance to integrate their birthmother role with a positive sense of self-worth.

Preface

A Note from the Authors

Over the past thirteen years, we have collectively shepherded more than five hundred adoptions along the path to completion. A vast majority of those adoptions have been "open" adoptions, where the biological or "birth" mother and sometimes her partner and family have participated in selecting new parents for the child.

Adoption has changed tremendously in the last few decades. Where secrecy and shame about the adoption decision were once the norm, openness and pride now exist. We believe the changes made since that time—when the word "adoption" was whispered and all decisions about the placement were made by social workers—have been for the best. This is not to say that open adoption is not subject to its own difficulties, but recognizing a child's true history undoubtedly gives children a more complete understanding of who they are.

The benefits are most evident for the birthparents. Birthmothers tell us repeatedly how comforting it is to know their child has been welcomed and is deeply loved in his or her new family. And, in many open adoptions where the relationship between the birth and adoptive families continues over the years, the birthparents are further reassured that the child remains happy and healthy.

While each adoption is unique, there is a range of common experiences shared by those who decide to place their child for adoption. When we are working with women and their partners who are trying to decide if adoption is right for them, or who have already decided to place their child for adoption, we hear the same questions over and over again. "How do I know if I am doing the right thing?" "What are my rights?" "Is what I am feeling normal?" "What happens next?" Of course, there are no pat answers, but through the hundreds of birthmothers, fathers, and families with whom we have worked, we have seen common themes emerge. We hope to share this information with you and provide the tools that may help with the decisions you will face along the way.

We had many compelling reasons prompting us to write the first edition of this book. For starters, Leslie was seeing many post-adoption birthmothers in her psychotherapy practice coming to therapy for help with depression, anxiety, relationship and intimacy issues, body image issues, chemical dependency and self-loathing. These women differed in many ways. Some were in their 20's and some were grandmothers; some were married and some were single; some were mothers again and some were childless. The stories they told began to form a single thread. When they faced an untimely pregnancy, they felt as though the fate of their pregnancy and eventually the course of their lives was out of their control. They did not feel they had unconditional support to think carefully about their options and to craft the outcome of their pregnancies. They were unclear about what was best for themselves and for their baby. This powerlessness, lack of control and untapped grief, disguised as psychological problems, came back to haunt many of these women.

A second reason for creating *The Third Choice* became apparent when we worked as counselors in an agency facilitating open adoptions. We were always scrambling to find literature that we could send home with women intending to place their child for adoption. There were few books about the grieving process in general and even fewer books about adoption written for birthmothers. We found ourselves going to the copy machine, making copies of a few well-written articles to try to inform these women about the birthmother experience.

While the adoption sections of bookstores and catalogues were growing furiously with books intended for prospective adoptive parents, adoptive parents and children, and adult adoptees, there was virtually nothing written for the birthparent audience about the nuts and bolts of the adoption process itself. We wanted to give our birthmothers information, support and courage. We wanted to encourage these women to feel empowered to help create an adoption situation they could live with. We interviewed post adoption birthmothers and asked them what they needed both pre- and post-adoption, and what they wished they had gotten.

After the first edition of our book came out in 1999, we knew we had filled a need for women both pre- and post-adoption. The feedback we received was overwhelmingly positive. Most notably, agencies, attorneys and facilitators bought our book to give to the birthmothers they were working with. Adoptive parents commented that our book helped them understand the birthparents' feelings and perspectives as well.

We also received feedback about portions of our book that needed more depth. We decided to work on a second edition of *The Third Choice* to make sure that it was as up to date and thorough as possible. We added many more concepts, deepened the ideas that we began in the first edition, and attempted to round out the chapters with a comprehensive resource guide. We hope that readers everywhere will find what they need in our new edition.

The decision to place a child for adoption is a very difficult and personal one. While some like to put a political spin on adoption, this is not our purpose, desire, or intent. We do not advocate adoption over other options you may be considering. We believe each woman in each situation needs to decide for herself, and the best decisions include information about all options. Adoption can be a very satisfying choice, and we hope any woman who chooses it will do so with pride and dignity.

This book was written with the help of the many birthmothers, birthfathers, and birthfamilies who so graciously shared their experiences, thoughts, and feelings with us. In many cases, we have used their own words to illustrate a point. This book is not to be confused with a research project, though. It is simply a compilation of personal observations added to our firsthand experience as adoption counselors.

Although we use the term "birthmother" throughout this book, we want to emphasize that an expectant mother is not a birhtmother until after her child is legally adopted.

We struggled to find the right title for our book. In our work as adoption counselors, women told us that while abortion and parenting were discussed as possible outcomes to their untimely pregnancies, the choice of adoption was much less frequently explored. It is our intention to include placing a child for adoption among options, as one of three possible choices, not a last choice.

We see this book as a guide for those who are considering placing a child for adoption, as well as for those who have already made that decision. You will hear the words of others who have been in your position, and perhaps you will even hear your own thoughts reflected in those of another and feel comforted knowing you are not alone.

Chapter 1:
CHOOSING ADOPTION

A Personal Choice

Men and women, whether young or old, single or married, financially stable or struggling, childless or parenting, will choose adoption in response to an untimely pregnancy. The life situations that contribute to this difficult decision are as varied as the people themselves. Choosing adoption instead of abortion or opting to parent is **a very personal choice.** Advice may be gathered from friends and family, questions can be answered by professionals or others who have gone before you, but ultimately the decision must be yours. No one really knows what it's like to be in your shoes, and no one really knows what is right for you.

Rhonda was seventeen years old and a junior in high school when she first found out she was pregnant. She was active in her local 4-H club, was planning to apply to college, and had recently broken up with the father of her unborn child. Although her parents would have supported her if she wanted to parent the baby, Rhonda chose adoption so she could continue growing up herself and so her baby would have the kind of life she was not in a position to provide.

Kathleen and Ron, both thirty-two, had been married for seven years and had three children. Their relationship became very rocky when Ron started to feel the increasing pressure of having to financially support his family and Kathleen began to feel more and more removed from the world outside her home. Ron worked incessantly, Kathleen felt unfulfilled, and their communication deteriorated. Soon, Kathleen was pregnant with another man's child. Stunned and confused, the couple began marriage counseling, and with the help of their therapist, decided adoption would be their best choice.

Pauline was a single, thirty-six-year-old law student working part time in a law firm. She had taken some time off from her education but was now committed to finishing school and taking the bar exam. She had never thought of herself as a mother, so when she discovered that her birth control had failed her, she was devastated and conflicted. After much thought, Pauline chose adoption because she knew of many couples who desperately wanted to adopt. The father agreed with her decision and participated in the adoption plan, although the two of them were no longer dating.

Stephanie was twenty-one years old and the single mother of Tiffany, a beautiful two-and-a-half-year-old little girl. Stephanie did not receive any help financially or emotionally from Tiffany's father, so she had been living on AFDC. She had hoped to return to trade school and become a respiratory therapist once Tiffany began kindergarten, so it was overwhelming to face the prospect of another unplanned pregnancy. Her relationship with Curtis, the father, was fairly new, and for both financial and emotional reasons, they decided to place their child for adoption.

Reasons for Choosing Adoption

One of the most common reasons for placing a child for adoption is feeling unprepared emotionally to parent a child at this time or under these circumstances. You might have personal dreams or goals that feel more pressing. Or you may wish to be in a committed relationship or marriage before starting or adding to your family. Some birthparents say they feel burdened by unresolved feelings from their own childhood that they would like to explore and address before becoming a parent.

"I was raised in a series of foster homes, with occasional visits from my mother. Her life was pretty screwed up, so I never knew what it was like to have a stable parent. I don't even know how to be a mother. I want something better for my baby."

While some women have the support and help of the birthfather in making their decision or following through with their adoption plan, oftentimes birthmothers are on their own. The likelihood of being a single parent dissuades many women from parenting. This is especially true when birthmothers already have one or more children. They know what it is like to be a single parent and feel overwhelmed at the prospect of caring for another child alone.

> *"I was already the single parent of a three-year-old, and I knew I couldn't raise two by myself. I felt like we would all be shortchanged: I would feel stressed and stretched way too thin, my daughter wouldn't get enough of me, and the baby wouldn't get what he needed either."*

Sometimes unplanned pregnancies occur in very new relationships, and many times the birthparents will use their own experiences as children or their parents' experiences to help them make their decision.

> *When Dianna became pregnant, she and Rick had only been together for six months. Both felt their relationship was too unstable and new to commit to raising a child together, and neither felt comfortable with abortion. Dianna knew her mother and father had married when pregnant with her older brother, and she decided she wanted to begin her family feeling more prepared.*

It is not uncommon for some birthmoms to know they never really wanted to be mothers. They feel different from some of their friends who fully anticipate motherhood. They may have pursued a meaningful career while their friends were having babies. These women have had very full and satisfying lives, with or without a partner, and do not plan on having a child.

In some communities, placing a child for adoption is a very unpopular choice. For example, some young women facing an unplanned pregnancy are encouraged to have an abortion or to keep their babies. The pressure can come from their families, their peer groups, or their high schools. While abortion and teen parenting are widely discussed in the media, adoption is the option least considered. For these reasons, making an adoption plan can be a particularly difficult decision for a teen. Most students attending teen parent programs do not consider adoption, so those who do may feel differently from their friends and unsupported. Young birthmothers usually cite wanting to finish their education and wanting to be married as reasons for adoption. They may have seen friends who chose to parent early facing the difficult realities of caring for a baby. They want something different for their lives.

> *"In my PAPT Program (pregnant and parenting teen), I am the only one who put my child up for adoption. A lot of my friends said, 'How can you give up your child?' or they'd say, 'You made your bed, now lie in it!' but I knew I was doing the responsible thing. I could see how they were having a hard time just getting by."*

When a child is conceived through rape, incest, or as part of a violent relationship, adoption can be considered as a way of partially severing the connection to the birthfather. Circumstances such as these can be extremely painful and emotionally complicated. It is strongly advised that professional guidance be sought to help sort through the confusion that will naturally occur under these conditions.

How Do I Know If Adoption Is Right for Me?

The reasons for choosing adoption over other options are quite varied, personal, and complicated. How do you begin to explore whether it is the right choice for you? You can start by looking at your feelings the moment you found out you were pregnant.

> *"When I first found out, I was mortified. As soon as I walked out of the clinic after finding out I was too far along to terminate the pregnancy, adoption was the first word out of my mouth."*

> *"I was scared and excited at the same time. I was scared because I had no idea what to expect but also really excited about being pregnant and having a life growing inside of me. I kept asking myself, 'Am I parent material?' "*

If you are unsure about adoption, we encourage you to take time to consider all the options available to you. Each choice carries with it lifelong consequences, involving not only your future, but also the future of another individual—your child. Rather than limiting your consideration to how the decision will affect your life right now, it is very helpful to imagine what your life will look like in the future with each of your options.

Choosing to Parent

Who doesn't love babies? They're designed to be adorable. And when they look at you as if you were the most important and wonderful thing in their universe (and you are), the thoughts about being a mom are almost irresistible. If you have never been a mom, this is likely to be your image of parenting. If you are a parent, or even if you have little brothers and sisters, you know that parenting is so much more than this. Parenting means that from this day forward, your desires and needs and personal goals will never again be number one. Are you ready for this lifelong responsibility?

Talk to some new moms in order to get a realistic picture in your mind of what parenting an infant is really like. Better yet, spend a few days with them. Try to picture yourself doing these things with a baby. Ask the parents of toddlers what they think has been the most rewarding and the most difficult part of parenting. Begin to observe young children in public places. Imagine what you will do to support yourself and your child. Ask yourself questions. Will you work? Go to school? Is there public assistance in your area? How much financial assistance can you expect? What will your income be? What expenses will you have—rent, utilities, phone, formula, diapers, food? Can you afford to live on your own? If you plan to work or go to school, who will care for your child during these times? How much will that cost? Does that fit your budget? What will happen when your baby gets sick? Can you take time off work? Do you have support to care for your baby from the birthfather and/or your family? Call around inquiring about the availability and cost of infant and childcare.

Take the time to reflect on what it felt like when you were a child. What were the things you cherished about the way you were raised? What were the things you desperately needed but did not get? What are your hopes and dreams for this child? Are you in a position to provide the kinds of experiences you believe will contribute to your child's healthy self-esteem?

We encourage you to explore the option of parenting, even if you are leaning toward abortion or adoption. When we receive calls from women who have never had a baby before and they tell us firmly that they are one hundred percent sure adoption is right for them, we are immediately concerned. In very early pregnancy, the baby often does not seem real. As the pregnancy progresses and you begin to feel the baby growing and kicking, you might feel a rush of emotion. Reality sets in. It is at this point that you might reconsider your adoption decision.

Abortion

Nicolette was a twenty-two-year-old single mother of a five-year-old. When she became pregnant at the age of seventeen, she never for a moment considered abortion; it went against her strict Christian upbringing. So, even though she was unmarried, she chose to have her son. Finding herself pregnant again when her son was only two years old, she knew she could not parent another child as a single mom. Raising Sonny was just about more than she could take, with what little she got from welfare and without family support. Reluctantly, she chose adoption and placed her son with a loving Christian family. It was only a year after that when she found herself pregnant once again. She had been proud of her adoption decision, but it had taken a tremendous emotional commitment on her part. She didn't think she could do it again, and this time she chose abortion. She worried how she would feel about herself afterward. She was not proud of her choice, but even after her abortion, she felt she had done the right thing and could live with all her decisions.

Is abortion an option you are considering? If so, you must first find out if you are eligible for one. Get a full examination, including a pregnancy test, a physical exam, and an ultrasound (if recommended), to make sure you are pregnant and to determine exactly how far along you are in your pregnancy. Some women who might consider abortion if they were eight weeks pregnant would not consider it knowing they were further along. You will also need to be screened for any potential health conditions you may have that would either prohibit you from safely having an abortion or add to the risk of the procedure. This is very important. Even though abortions are performed into the second trimester, you may find you are not a candidate due to health reasons.

Also, an abortion may not be available in your region, or the cost may prohibit you from seeking one.

You may also want to find out if there are any legal barriers to seeking abortion. Some states require a 24-hour waiting period between a counseling session and the abortion procedure. Other states require a minor to notify or get the consent of their parents or custodial guardian prior to being granted an abortion. However, for most women aged eighteen or over, the abortion decision is private and confidential, made between them and their health care provider.

If abortion is an option for you, yet you are still unsure, we encourage you to take the time you need to explore your own personal value system as it relates to this very important decision. Ask yourself:

- Could you live with and accept the fact that you had an abortion?
- What are your family's beliefs about abortion?
- Do you have religious or personal beliefs that support or condemn abortion?
- If your values and beliefs have always been that abortion is wrong, and now you find yourself considering it, how will you feel about yourself after the abortion?
- Do you have friends or family members who will support your decision to have an abortion regardless of their own views?

The issue of abortion is highly emotional and evokes volatile public debate. It is also a personal and private decision. Opinions vary widely. Each woman experiences this decision and its aftermath differently. Some women say they felt incredibly sad and took a long time to forgive themselves; others say they experienced immediate relief from the burden of the unwanted pregnancy and were grateful to have had the choice. Most women have mixed feelings about this choice, both before and after an abortion, but they are able to live with their decision. Some feel they have betrayed their own beliefs about abortion and are left feeling spiritually drained. There is no way to *absolutely* predict how you will feel if you do choose abortion. If you are considering this choice, it is advisable to see a counselor. Many health clinics and women's clinics have counselors who will provide you with non-biased, choice counseling. Talking to other women who have had abortions can also be extremely helpful.

If You Are Seriously Considering Adoption

If you decide adoption is the best choice, you need to explore how you will be able to carry out and live with the decision. Many women find that, while they believe their adoption decision is a good one for them and for their child, they have a difficult time facing up to the reality of their decision and the associated emotions. We have found that it is extremely helpful to explore your thoughts, feelings and choices before proceeding with an adoption plan. In fact, most women do not actually move forward with an adoption plan until the last few months of pregnancy. By that time, abortion is no longer a practical option, and the decision has been narrowed to parenting or adoption. The further along in the pregnancy you are, the more real the baby is. The baby is kicking and turning and making herself known, and thoughts of parenting or placing the baby for adoption are more deeply felt.

Most women who chose adoption say they thought about it almost immediately when they learned they were pregnant but did nothing to act on it until later in the pregnancy because they were still unsure. Thank goodness for a nine-month pregnancy! It gives you time to think it over. As you approach the birth of your baby, especially as you enter your last trimester (the last three months), you will have time to think about actually placing the baby with an adoptive family.

When they are able to envision the tough parts of an adoption decision, most women start the process of grieving and "letting go" which is essential to any adoption. When considering adoption:

- Picture yourself carrying a baby full-term but not taking that baby home from the hospital.
- Think about the type of parents you can envision for your child. Can you imagine someone other than yourself being mom?
- Imagine returning to your life having given birth but not being seen by the world as a mother.
- Think about being connected to this child in one way or another over the years, even if you don't see or hear from the child.
- If you are in a relationship with the birthfather, reflect on how you see your relationship after you place the baby for adoption.

Now check in with yourself. How does it feel to picture yourself in these various scenes? Acknowledging the personal difficulty of this decision will help you prepare for it and find ways to gather strength in the months ahead. Women we have worked with who refused to look at their feelings or who denied there would be any difficulty often had the most painful post-adoption recovery. Even though your decision to place your child for adoption is "right" for you, it does not mean you will not feel sad. And remember, you do not have to decide the outcome of your pregnancy today.

Sarah was a thirty-two-year-old graphic designer who felt pressured to decide how to handle her unplanned pregnancy. Her current boyfriend was not the father of her baby, and she felt compelled to hurry up and eliminate the tension in her new relationship. She chose to do an open adoption during her eighth week of pregnancy and had met and connected with a couple before the end of her first trimester. In retrospect, Sarah wished her counselor had encouraged her to slow down and take more time to decide.

Even if you are due to deliver in one week, it is very important for you to be able to sit with your decision for a while until you have "tried it on" and are sure that it fits.

"I wish someone had told me it wouldn't kill me just to sit with my feelings for a little while. I was so anxious that I thought just making a decision would feel better. It did for a while, but as the pregnancy progressed and I began to feel the baby move inside of me, I realized that in my rush to decide, I had avoided a lot of the feelings I had toward the baby."

Who Chooses Open Adoption?

As you explore the idea of placing your child for adoption, be aware of any preconceived ideas you have about adoption in general or any stereotypes you have about what birthparents are like or about what kind of people would "give up their child." If you have formed your ideas based on movies or on other people's experiences, or if you yourself were raised in the foster system, you may need to reexamine adoption in light of today's options for openness. For so long, adoption was conducted in secrecy, and therefore an inordinate amount of shame was attached to the idea. This was true for birthparents, who may have been perceived as "promiscuous" or "rejecting"; for adoptive parents, who were "barren"; and for adoptees, who were "given away." Quite the contrary, the authors view birthparents as selfless, courageous, and loving people. However, your own unspoken or unconscious attitudes toward birthparents may influence your decision or impact the way you feel about yourself.

One thing to remember is that your experiences, feelings, thoughts, and circumstances are unique to you. It can be very helpful to solicit feedback from people you can trust with your dilemma, but ultimately your values will be the most important to examine.

Is Adoption My Decision Alone?

While you have the main rights to the child you wish to place for adoption, there are others who have the right and the power to keep you from doing so. Of course, the most important person is the biological father of the child, whose rights are equal to yours in most cases. If you are American Indian, you may also be subject to the Indian Child Welfare Act, which places your child under the jurisdiction of a tribal council. If you are under legal guardianship, you may have to get permission from your guardian. The grandparents of the child (your parents or the birthfather's parents) do not have legal rights to block an adoption unless the grandparents have developed a significant relationship with the child or have parented the child for you. In this case, the grandparents may be able to get the court to give them the authority to care for the child.

Telling the Birthfather

The father of the baby has important rights in the adoption decision. This means that if you want to pursue adoption, and the father objects or contests, you may not be able to place your child for adoption. It is important to let the father of the baby know early on about the pregnancy and your interest in adoption. We have found that most men in this position will agree with your adoption plan when they are included in the decision-making process. It is not a good idea to try to hide your adoption plans from the birthfather for several reasons. The first and obviously the most important one is that he has a right to know about a child he has fathered. Secondly, if you are seriously considering adoption, his cooperation and emotional support may be helpful. Lastly, without the birthfather's consent, the legalization of the adoption may not be completed. If you knowingly keep your pregnancy and adoption plans from the legal father of the baby, he can challenge the adoption and could even take the child away from the adoptive parents in the years to come.

There are different categories to determine the legal father of a child. If you are married, separated, or very recently divorced, your husband (or ex-husband) is legally the father of your baby, whether or not he is the actual biological father. This is not an uncommon occurrence, and birthmothers in these situations must get the consent of both the husband or ex-husband and the biological father.

In many states, the biological father's rights may be equal to yours, even if you are not married to him, and you may need to get his consent to the adoption. While there are situations where the birthfather does not have the same rights as you, it is becoming common practice to treat all potential birthfathers as if they were the legal fathers and had equal rights to the child. We have increasingly seen the rights of birthfathers upheld, resulting in cases where an adoption was overturned, even when the child was as old as five. To avoid this, we recommend that all potential birthfathers be treated as if they had one hundred percent equal rights to the child. Since this is a legal issue, we suggest you consult an adoption attorney to answer your questions about birthfather rights.

If you have had sexual intercourse with more than one partner around the time of conception, a consent must be obtained from each person since you cannot determine before the birth exactly who the father is. We have worked with an occasional birthmother and birthfather who wanted to be absolutely sure who the biological father of the baby was and arranged to have genetic testing done to determine paternity. For this procedure, you must have blood from the mother, father, and child. The testing must be done after the baby is born, and most tests take about six weeks for the results.

Telling Family and Friends

In most cases, you have no legal obligation to tell your family about your pregnancy or about your intentions to place the baby for adoption. If you are a minor, you should ask an attorney or agency representative about the laws in your particular state. Some states do require a minor birthmother to be represented by an adult guardian when she signs the relinquishment, releasing her legal right to the child.

It is an entirely personal decision whether or not you want to tell family or friends about your pregnancy and adoption interest or intentions. If you are fifteen and live at home with your parents, you have a very different obligation to your family than if you are an adult woman living on your own and supporting yourself. If you are seriously considering adoption, we encourage you to confide in close friends or family members who can help you sort through your situation, or whose opinion might significantly influence your decision should they find out about your pregnancy and plans. All too often we have worked with women pursuing adoption, particularly young women, whose intention was to keep the entire pregnancy and adoption a secret from family, and who changed their minds when their family found out about the pregnancy. This is absolutely tragic when it occurs after an adoption plan has been made, the adoptive family picked, and the baby placed.

If you are reasonably certain an adoption is what you want, and you are afraid to tell your family because you think they will disapprove and try to talk you out of it, find a trusted friend, counselor, teacher, or member of the clergy who can come with you to talk to your family. It is possible that your family will not immediately embrace your plans. While you have had days, weeks, or perhaps months to get used to the fact of your pregnancy and to move emotionally through your options, your family will be hearing about it for the first time. Remember how panicked you felt when you first found out you were pregnant. Give them a little breathing space. They will have a lot to think about, too. While it is ultimately your decision, this is a child they will also be losing should you choose adoption.

If you are thinking about open adoption, this may be a new concept to your family. Birthgrandparents may be more comfortable with and even supportive of their son or daughter's adoption decision if they know that they may be able to meet the adopting parents and have an ongoing relationship with the parents and the child over their lifetimes.

Financial Support and Living Accommodations

Some women considering adoption have a very real need for financial support during their pregnancy, including options for different living accommodations. All states allow expectant mothers to receive, directly or indirectly, support for pregnancy-related expenses. The extent of this support varies widely, though. In some states, expectant mothers can only receive support for the pregnancy-related health care provided to them and their baby, and only if an agency acts as the intermediary financial governor of these reimbursements. Other states allow not only pregnancy-related health care, but also living expenses and other support. No states allow general payments to the parents-to-be that are unrelated to the pregnancy or adoption. Any payments, which cannot be directly linked to the pregnancy or legitimate adoption costs, can be misconstrued as a payment for the child, which is illegal.

Before you make any financial arrangements regarding support during your pregnancy or after, we recommend you either consult with an adoption agency or with an attorney familiar with adoption practice in your state and in the state of the adopting family.

Just How Sure Do I Have to Be?

It is completely normal to go back and forth when deciding if adoption is the right choice for you, throughout your pregnancy and even beyond. Many women have reported they were waiting for the time they felt "one hundred percent sure" of their decision. For some birthparents, this is realistic, but for others, "sureness" is more fluid. It is natural to reevaluate your decision time and time again. Part of this process may involve acknowledging that you actually feel ambiguity about the pregnancy, the baby, or how to proceed. This does not necessarily mean that you have made the wrong choice or that you will change your mind. It simply means that choosing adoption is a very difficult and complicated decision that, by its very nature, involves conflict.

One birthmother compared choosing adoption to trying to break off a destructive relationship with her boyfriend:

"Throughout my pregnancy, I kept thinking about the time I

struggled to break up with Dayle. I loved him so much, and we'd been together so long, that leaving him felt like a death. But I knew that the relationship was hurting me, and that staying with him was not doing either of us any good. I guess this felt like another example of choosing short-term pain for what I believed was the better good."

Chapter 2:
CHOOSING THE RIGHT
ADOPTION FOR YOU

*For some women, finding the right kind of adoption
is central to the adoption decision itself.*

How to Decide on the Right Adoption Plan for You

Women who never considered adoption as an option before
might feel differently if they could have an open adoption. Other
women who prefer to have a more closed adoption, at least initially,
will benefit if there remains an option for openness later on in life.

*"For me, it really made a difference in whether or not I would
place my son for adoption—knowing where he was going
and who his parents were going to be helped me feel safe."*

*"Even though I knew my decision was right, I just couldn't
bring myself to get involved with selecting and meeting the
parents. I really trusted my adoption counselors to tell me
everything I wanted to know, but I just had to keep my mind
on getting back to my life. I like that I have the option to find
out how my child is doing later on, when I am more ready.
That feels good, but for right now, it is just too hard."*

Although there have been a lot of changes in adoption since the early 1980s, there are still many parts of the country where all adoption options are not available. When open adoptions first became available, some women had to contact adoption centers or attorneys outside their geographical area to find professionals who offered openness as an option. We were amazed, at first, that these women would be willing to place their children with a family so far from their own home, that they would travel so many miles from their loved ones in order to have an open adoption. As we counseled these women, we learned that, for them, placing their child with a family thousands of miles from their home in an open adoption was better than having a closed adoption in their own backyard! After all, what good is having your birthchild nearby if you can never hear from or see the child anyway?

Closed Adoption

In a truly closed adoption, neither the birthparents nor the adopting parents have any identifying information about one another. A social worker usually arranges all of the aspects of the adoption. Typically, the adoptive family will be chosen by the social worker and an adoption agency, as the birthparent is not allowed to participate in the selection process. In some cases, the agency will ask the birthmother what her wishes for a couple are, and those wishes may be taken into consideration when the selection is made. The adopting parents are not allowed information about the birthfamily except for any health, medical, or social history which is deemed relevant. Most people who were adopted in this country prior to the 1980s were not given complete and accurate medical information about their birthfamilies and now must go through lengthy legal procedures or costly investigative searches to find the information about their origins.

In most states, closed adoption records are sealed and cannot be opened except in special circumstances, such as a medical emergency, or when the adoptee has reached legal age (usually eighteen) and all parties agree. Many adult adoptees have been unable to access information about their birth and heritage and many birthparents are, to this day, unable to find out about the children they placed for adoption years ago.

Open Adoption

Open adoptions, on the other hand, are characterized by a full sharing of information between the birth and adoptive parents and ongoing contact between the child and the birthfamily. In an open adoption, the birthparents are typically given a number of eligible prospective parents to choose from. The information available to the birthparents often includes pictures of the adoptive parents, their full names, ages, place of residence, marital status and length of marriage, whether or not they have other children, and so forth. Birthparents then have the opportunity to review the "resumes" of prospective parents until they find ones they would like to meet. Upon meeting, both parties gather more information about one another and can ask questions about their wishes for ongoing contact to see if their desires are compatible. Usually the birth and adoptive families continue to stay in touch long after the adoption itself is completed, and many birth and adoptive parents consider each other to be "extended family."

"I was scared about how I might feel, seeing my baby with her new parents in their home for the first time. I didn't know if I would be jealous, or if I would just want to take her home with me, or what. But it really helped. I saw how much the parents loved her, and I could picture what her life was going to be like. It's what I wanted for her. I knew that day I had made the right decision."

Some early critics of open adoption expressed concern that birthmothers would not be able to handle the ongoing relationship with their birthchild and that the openness would make it more difficult to separate from the child. In general, we have not found this to be true. As a matter of fact, in the vast majority of open adoptions in which we are involved, birthmothers are actually able to separate more easily because they can see for themselves that the child is safe and happy and that the adopting parents love the child as their own.

One birthmother describes her adoption this way:

"The adoptive parents have become like family to me. We talk or e-mail one to two times each month. They send pictures of "our daughter" at every stage. I send letters and

cards at least once a month. The adoptive parents have eased my fears by letting me set the pace and always letting me know what a gift I've given them. We get together a few times a year. I have given my daughter a wonderful life with everything she could want. And I know that I found the perfect mom and dad for her because they love her just like I do."

Semi-Open Adoption

Many adoption facilitators making the transition from years of practicing closed adoption to the now more popular open adoption are practicing "semi-open" adoption. This type of adoption borrows from both closed and open adoption in that the birth and adoptive families may meet and even share information about themselves, but most contact is controlled and coordinated through the adoption agency. Identifying information, such as addresses, last names, and phone numbers, is not disclosed, and ongoing contact is usually by letter, via the adoption facilitator.

Many people who engage in a semi-open adoption "open up" their adoption on their own by sharing more information directly with one another, without agency mediation. If both families are comfortable with each other, they can then proceed on their own.

Agency Adoption

An adoption agency may be either a public (state or county) or private (religious or social service) organization that is licensed to approve prospective parents for the purpose of adoption. An agency also places babies or children in those homes after taking a legal relinquishment of rights from the birthparents. Adoption agencies provide counseling before and after the child is born. Each agency has its own unique protocol governing how much it will allow the birthparents to participate in the adoption process and the selection of parents for the child. Some agencies are very strict and do not allow the birth and adopting parents to have any identifying information about each other, nor do they permit meetings or ongoing contact. Other agencies will allow some information to be shared between parties (letters, pictures, etc.) but will control the type of information and contact allowed. Still other agencies will not only allow but will encourage the birthparents to select the adopting parents from their pool of approved applicants. Such agencies often support an ongoing relationship among all parties.

With agency adoptions, all adopting parents are pre-approved through an investigative process called a home study (see "Elements of a Home Study," Chapter 3). Birthparents are usually expected to sign all final adoption papers, called relinquishments, a short time after the child is born and either placed in temporary foster care or with the adoptive family. State laws vary as to when the relinquishment must be signed and whether or not the relinquishment may, at any time after, be revoked.

With this type of adoption, the birthparents must be very careful to ask questions about the relinquishment process in their particular adoption. In relinquishment (agency) adoptions, the birthmother releases custody of the child to the agency, which then places the child in an adoptive home. Many agencies will do "designated adoptions," offering birthparents a greater measure of control by allowing them to place the baby directly with the adoptive parents of their choosing.

Identified or Designated Adoption

Some birth and adopting parents come together on their own but decide to work through an agency to complete their adoption. These adoptions are really agency adoptions that simply did not rely on the agency to match them up. In an identified or designated adoption, the birthmother can go through a cooperating agency and designate with whom she wants her child to be placed. This option is also recommended by agencies that encourage birthmothers to take an active part in selecting the family that is right for her and her baby. This allows the birthmother to have complete control over where the child goes, rather than risk leaving the decision in the hands of the agency.

Independent or Private Adoption

Independent or private adoption allows birthparents to choose adoptive parents on their own. Many birthparents turned to independent adoption, particularly in the '80s and early '90s, because most agencies did not allow fully open adoption. Independent adoption, which is controlled only by the participants, sometimes offers more options and flexibility. Independent adoptions are regulated differently than agency adoptions, though, and while many of those in the independent adoption field (like attorneys, facilitators, and counselors) are committed to high-quality service and ethical practice, it is up to the birth and adopting parents to check out the reputation of any providers with whom they may work.

Most states allow independent adoption, but laws do vary from state to state. In all states where independent adoption is practiced, the adopting parents will be required to submit to a home study (as in agency adoption) prior to the finalization of the adoption. The home study is completed by a social worker from state social services or in some cases by a social worker from a private agency. In independent adoption, the home study is usually not completed until after the baby has been placed with the adoptive parents. An attorney will handle the legal aspects, paid for by the adoptive parents, and the birthmother is entitled to her legal counsel as well.

Foster Care

Foster care is a short-term home for children whose parents are temporarily unable to care for them. Adoption agencies usually have foster homes that are licensed and approved by the state or county. When a woman is not sure if she wants to place her child for adoption, foster care can be a way to have separation from the child while deciding. If you do decide to place your child in temporary foster care, make sure you know exactly what is involved. How long can the baby stay? What are the legal requirements? What papers will you have to sign? What will you have to do to take your baby out of foster care? As an alternative to foster care, some women have asked a family member or close friend to care for their baby, so they can have some time and space to make their decision.

Choosing the Right Adoption for You and Your Child

Now that you know what options are available, you may already know which type of adoption fits you best. At first, many women are unsure about whether or not they want an open adoption. An unplanned pregnancy is very stressful, and the decision to place a child for adoption is usually very difficult. At this point, some women feel it would be a relief to let someone else make the decisions for them. Others feel they don't have the skills or intuition to pick suitable parents. Still others choose closed adoption because they are afraid contact with the family or the child will be too difficult for them emotionally, or because they just don't want the responsibility of developing a relationship with an adopting couple.

We have found that most women who initially choose a closed adoption will decide sometime later in the process that they want more participation than they originally thought. For example, they may want to hear more about the adoptive parents, see a picture of the child, or meet the family. They also may decide they would like to know about the child at some point later on in life.

If you are considering a closed adoption, we encourage you to select an adoption professional who can also offer you more openness should you change your mind at any point along the way. You can do this either through a supportive agency or with an independent adoption practitioner, attorney, or counselor.

Selecting an Adoption Facilitator

Once you decide on the type of adoption you want, you will need someone who can help you through the adoption process-someone who can advise you of your rights, help you locate an adoptive couple, give you emotional support, guide you through the ups and downs, and advocate for you. In finding the right person to help you through this maze of choices, there are a few options available. You can work with a licensed adoption agency in your area, public or private. You can work with an independent facilitator, usually a counselor, attorney, or non-profit organization, or you may decide to find a family for your child on your own through a network of friends and relations.

Most birthmothers are less concerned about whether they choose an agency or an independent adoption than they are about getting the type of adoption program they want and being treated with care and respect. There are many ways to find the right program for you. You can ask your doctor, family lawyer, social worker, local social service agency, nurses at the hospital, family planning clinic, school nurse, counselor, or member of the clergy. These are generally good places to start because many of these professionals have had experience with local adoption providers and can recommend a good program.

You can also look in the yellow pages of the phone book or through the "personals" section of some newspaper want ads. Many independent practitioners, attorneys, agencies and individual families now have sites on the Internet. We recommend you call several adoption providers to get information before deciding on a program.

Call for Information

Make a list of questions that are important to you before you call, and leave a space to write down the answers and your general impressions. You will begin to get an idea about the philosophy and services of each provider, as well as their general character. No matter what kind of adoption you feel is right for you, you will want to find an organization that believes in your right to make decisions about how you would like your adoption to proceed. And just as important, you will need to find a place that will advocate for and support you through this process from beginning to end.

Sample Questions for an Adoption Facilitator or Agency

- What type of adoptions do you typically facilitate? If they say, open adoption, have them define, "open."
- Can I choose the parents myself?
- Do you have any restrictions on the type of families I can choose from? (i.e. Do you have single parents or gay and lesbian families? Can I choose a family of a different ethnicity?)
- Do you provide counseling? If so, how long after the birth can I receive counseling?
- How soon after the birth or the actual placement do I sign my relinquishment or consent to the adoption?

- How long does it take for the adoption to be finalized?
- Can I place my baby directly with adoptive parents? Will my baby have to go into foster care first?
- Can I place my baby with parents in a different state?
- What expenses are allowed (i.e. counseling, medical expenses, living expenses)?
- What is the relinquishment process for the birthfather? When does he sign his consent or relinquishment?
- Do you have a birthparent support group or other birthparents I can talk to?

If You Cannot Find an Open Adoption Practitioner in Your Area

You must first find out if open adoption is available in your state or province. Ask the adoption agency that serves your area, an adoption attorney from the phone directory, or the Department of Social Services. If you cannot find an open adoption provider in your state, you may have to work with an agency in another state. If you and the adoptive parents you choose live in different states, you both must comply with the Interstate Compact for the Placement of Children (ICPC). The ICPC is an agreement between states, which allows for the legal placement of children from one state to another. Your agency or attorney will guide you through this process.

Chapter 3:
FINDING THE RIGHT ADOPTIVE PARENTS FOR YOUR CHILD

When considering the decision to place your child for adoption, the most important choice you will have to make is selecting the parents. Most birthmothers approach the decision with a mixture of nervousness, sadness, and excitement. Some women report feeling a lot of pressure. It can be scary to have such a big responsibility. It can also be a relief to finally have someone with whom to share your burden, someone who can actually find something joyous and wonderful about your pregnancy. Still, most birthparents ask themselves many questions: How will I know if these people will truly love my child? How can I be sure they will not abuse my child? What if I choose them and then find out they are not really who I thought they were? What will they think of me? What will they do if something is wrong with my baby? What if the adoptive parents I choose won't ever let me see my child? How can I be sure they will not get divorced? How will I know they are the right parents for my child?

These are all normal questions that most birthparents struggle with. They are also good questions to ask yourself before choosing the adoptive parent or parents for your child. There are other questions you must ask yourself as you approach this choice. Can I accept that anyone I choose will have human faults? Can I let go of my worry and doubt once I have selected them? Can I trust that this family will love and raise my child to the best of its ability?

Before You Choose Your Child's Parents

All adoption programs have different policies for selecting the adoptive parents. Some programs give you a choice of all the prospective parents they currently have waiting in their program, and others choose several couples they believe would be appropriate for you.

When adoptive parents join an adoption program, they are asked what type of child they hope to adopt. Factors such as the race and health of the birthparents or the potential prenatal exposure of the child to drugs, alcohol, or smoking are fundamentally important in determining a good match. If a couple has indicated it is only willing to adopt a child born to two Caucasian birthparents, for example, and you or the birthfather are not Caucasian, you should not have to waste your time considering them as parents. If you have used drugs or alcohol at any time during the pregnancy, and a certain couple in the program has indicated it is not willing to adopt a child exposed to these substances, then this is not the right couple for you or your child.

For these reasons, it is very important for you, as the birthmother, to be honest and forthright in letting your adoption counselor know everything before you start the process of selecting parents for your child. No matter what your circumstances, there is almost always an appropriate family available who will want to adopt your child. You have a greater chance of finding them if you are straightforward about your history and situation.

Getting Support from the Birthfather

For both legal and ethical reasons, it is important that the father of your baby be told about the pregnancy and about your desire to place the baby for adoption. Every state has different laws and practices regarding the rights of the father. It would be wise on your part to find out from a legal expert—an agency or attorney—exactly what the father's legal rights are in your state. For most birthmothers, involving the birthfather is not a problem. In fact, when an agreement about adoption can be reached between you and the birthfather, you may feel more confident and supported in your decision. Many birthmothers who have had the support of the birthfather have told us that his participation really made the difference.

Some birthmothers do not want to tell the birthfather about the pregnancy or the adoption plans. Sometimes there is good reason for this reluctance. Perhaps there has been violence in the relationship, or the pregnancy may have resulted from a coercive sexual experience. If this is the case, you need to discuss it with your counselor, who can help you sort through your emotions and your legal rights and protections.

Most often, a birthmother is reluctant to involve the birthfather because she does not want him to be part of her life anymore, or because she fears he will not consent to the adoption. It is important for the child, though, that the birthfather be notified. If the father is not notified, and at a later point—even years down the road—he finds out his child was placed for adoption without his knowledge or consent, he may have legal grounds to overturn the adoption. This would be a tragedy for your child. It is far better to find out now whether or not the birthfather will consent to the adoption, before you involve a potential adopting family.

The overwhelming reason the birthfather should be notified is so the child will have complete information regarding his history and know that his birthfather was part of the process. We recommend that birthfathers be welcomed into the decision-making and adoption-planning processes. If you are unwilling to notify the birthfather on your own about the pregnancy and adoption plan, your adoption facilitator, counselor, case worker, or attorney can help you by making the call or writing the letter to the father. We think that in most cases, the best approach is personal and direct contact from you. If you are nervous about this, ask the father to come with you to a counseling session so that your counselor can be there to help you both adjust to the situation together.

If You Are Not Sure Who the Birthfather Is

Sometimes birthmothers are not one hundred percent sure who the actual father of their baby is. This information is not only important ethically and legally, it can also make a difference in determining which adopting parents may be right for your child. If you are unsure who the father is and, as a result, are unsure of the race of the child or the child's health background, it is important to let your counselor know about your situation. That way the counselor can make sure you only receive information about the prospective parents who would be best suited for the child in any eventuality.

The Race of the Child and the Race of the Parents

All prospective parents are asked what race of child they would be interested in adopting. Laws and statutes in most states allow parents to adopt a child of a different race, particularly when the birthparents choose the couple and approve of the placement. Most experts in the field of child psychology and adoption agree that, all other things being equal, it is best for a child to have at least one parent who shares the child's race or ethnicity. However, that option is not always available. Unless the agency in which you are working has regulations against transracial adoptions, the decision is really up to you and the adoptive parents.

If you are considering placing your child in a family that does not share your child's racial or ethnic background, you should take some time to evaluate the potential long-term impact of this on your child's future. It is completely acceptable (and important!) to ask the prospective adopting parents questions about their thoughts, feelings, and plans on raising a child who does not share their racial background.

When we interview couples who express a desire to adopt transracially, we explore with them their ideas on how they will cope with the complexities of being a mixed-race family. Some couples indicate they will adopt a child of any race—just to become parents. We have commonly heard these prospective parents say, "A baby is a baby. We feel we can love a child of any race." While this may very well be true, parental love does not address the very real challenges the family will inevitably face from society.

As adoption counselors, we are encouraged when couples tell us they have put a lot of thought into adopting transracially and have discussed this with their important family members. We hope they will acknowledge the special challenges involved in adopting a child of a different race, while at the same time believing they can provide the child with a lifetime of support. When a Caucasian family adopts a child of color, for example, the fact that the child was adopted into that family becomes more evident and more public. The couple should be prepared to deal, as a family, with the fact that their adoption will come up more often than if the child shared their ethnicity.

The adopting parents must understand that their child's everyday experiences will be different from their own childhood experiences and take steps to learn how they can offer guidance and support to the child throughout his life. These parents will have created a transracial family, not just a transracial adoption.

QUESTIONS TO ASK ADOPTING PARENTS OF ANOTHER RACE

- Why did you decide to adopt a child of this race?
- How do you think you can help your child with issues of racism?
- What sort of things do you feel you can do to help this child deal with the fact that he or she is of a different ethnicity than you?
- Do you have any friends or family who are of the same race as the child?
- How do you plan to ensure that this child will feel proud of his or her race?
- How will you connect your child to people that share his/her racial heritage?
- Are you interested/willing to stay in touch with the birth parent with whom the child shares his or her predominant racial identity?
- How are you intending to stay connected to an adoption community that supports and provides education for transracial families?
- Do you plan to adopt other children? If so, will you adopt transracially?

There are no right or wrong answers to these questions, but the answers and discussion might give you insight into the way this particular couple is equipped to deal with the challenges of parenting, and what it means to them to become a transracial family through adoption.

Birthparents of American Indian Heritage

If you or the father of your child are of American Indian heritage, especially if you are registered with a tribe, you may not be able to freely choose adoption. The Indian Child Welfare Act (ICWA) was originally passed to protect Native American children from being removed and placed in non-Native homes. Tell your counselor right away if you or the birthfather are any part Native American. You must let them know what tribe or tribes you are affiliated with and any other relevant information. In these cases, the adoption workers must contact the tribe to make sure they will allow the adoption. Depending on your situation, the tribe may have jurisdiction over the child. This is very important, and if it is not done properly, your adoption could be jeopardized, even years later. To avoid any problems, let someone know right away so you can find out your rights and options.

Drugs, Alcohol, and Smoking

Any drug or alcohol use before or during your pregnancy should be revealed to your counselor. This does not mean your child is unadoptable. It is, however, something any prospective parent should know before they make a commitment to adopt your child. A fair number of adoptive parents are willing to consider adopting a child whose birthmother used drugs or alcohol during the pregnancy, as long as they have been told in advance. It is extremely difficult for adoptive parents to learn about drugs and alcohol usage at the hospital or afterward and can damage the trust in the relationship. You should also alert your counselor and adoptive parents if you smoke cigarettes.

Selecting the Adoptive Parents

You may have just one or two families to choose from, or you may have hundreds of families—it really depends on what type of program you are working with and what you are looking for. There are also a variety of ways adoption facilitators can involve you in the selection process. The most common approach these days is for prospective adoptive parents to write an introduction letter to a potential birthmother. You may have already seen one of these "birthmother letters" (see sample, below). This letter is typically one to two pages or more telling you about who they are, where they are from, and why they want to adopt. A picture or a collage of pictures of the family is glued or printed on the letter so that you can get an idea of what they look like and how they want to present themselves to you. These letters are a way to introduce the prospective parents to you and to let you know enough about them to get your interest.

Some programs will ask you to make a selection based on these letters. Very often, birthmothers will look through the letters and become drawn to a particular family, or they will find a few families they would like to learn more about.

Hello,

We are Kathy and Mike and hope this letter conveys our desire to provide a loving and caring home for your child. We find it hard to describe the depth of our desire to love and raise a child, and how completely that child will be cherished. We have seen that adoption can be a joyful process for everyone. Two of our nieces and nephews, David and Alissa, became part of our family through adoption. We cannot begin to tell you how totally loved they are and how completely they belong to all of us. Your choice to give your baby to a couple through adoption takes great courage and love. We respect you for taking this difficult path.

We own a cozy house in a small town 30 miles east of San Francisco. We have a large sunny back yard, perfect for a swing-set next to our hammock. Our town consists of 3 residential streets of primarily families with lots of children. There is a park with a playground 2 blocks from our home. The neighborhood houses are alive with holiday decorations. We can't wait to see our child's eyes light up when Santa Claus makes his special annual trip down each street passing out goodies for all the kids. There is a real sense of community here.

We have known each other for 12 years and have been married for 2 1/2 years. We both deeply love each other and our families and have always planned to have children. After 2 1/2 years of infertility we both realize that the most important thing to us is to become parents and to share our love and life with a child.

We believe that listening is a good foundation for parenting; children need to be respected for their feelings and opinions. We also believe that loving a child includes giving clear, consistent guidance and support to help in learning how to deal with life's ups and downs. We both strongly believe in a good education for our child. As parents we would encourage our child to develop self-esteem and support them in following whatever life path they choose.

It takes tremendous   of faith to
                                                of love,
your child.   doing so, our lives
entwined in   sense and you
will always be a valued and admired part of all
of our lives. If ours is the kind of family you
would like your baby to grow up in, please call

Benny plants a big wet   on Kathy.

Very Sincerely,

Kathy & Mike

Kathy & Mike Hamilton

In some very open adoption programs, these letters also include the family's home phone number so that you can call them up directly to talk. They also include the phone number of the adoption attorney or organization with whom the couple is working. You may call that number to find out more about the couple without talking to them directly.

Other programs offer information about the prospective parents without showing you their pictures or divulging any information about them that could identify them. This approach might appeal to some birthmothers who would prefer to read information about the families without seeing pictures so they do not feel influenced by physical appearance.

Getting More Information about the Adoptive Parents

You might want more information than is initially provided. It is your right to ask for as much information as you need in order to make a good decision. If you are working with a licensed agency, they will have a completed home study on the prospective parents, which will include all sorts of information: how long they have been married, religion, previous marriages, other children, their home environment, child discipline beliefs, whether or not they smoke, and their alcohol use. Besides the home study, adoption programs also have a more thorough and complete questionnaire on the prospective parents in their files, which they can share with you.

Beware of any person, organization, or agency that does not allow you to have this information. While most agencies will not simply hand over their confidential files to you, just as you would not expect your confidential information to be given to any adopting parent, they should be able to provide you with basic information and a summary of the home study findings.

ELEMENTS OF A HOME STUDY

1. Background Check
    Criminal record clearance
    Child abuse index clearance

2. Motivation and Readiness to Adopt
    Have infertility issues been explored?
    Is it a good time to add a child to the family, emotionally and
        financially?

3. Marriage Assessment
    Previous marriages
    Length and stability of marriage
    How do they deal with differences?

4. Individual Interviews
    Upbringing: childhood, adolescence, and adulthood
    Relationship with parents and siblings, past and present
    Autobiographies and questionnaires required at most agencies

5. Child Rearing Experiences
    How were they raised/disciplined?
    How do they plan to discipline?
    Experience with children
    Child-care plans

6. Finances
    Job security/satisfaction
    Income/assets

7. Type of Child Desired
    Age, ethnicity, handicaps
    Social worker's assessment of their strengths/limitations to
        parent

8. Adoption Issues
    How and when to tell a child about adoption
    How much openness do they want?
    Feelings toward birthparents
    Reading and workshops recommended to prepare for adoption

9. Religion
    Religious/spiritual upbringing
    Current spiritual beliefs and practices
    How will the child be raised?

10. Goals and Hobbies
    Educational values and aspirations for child
    Travel plans, career goals, and personal goals

11. Home Inspection for Health and Safety
    Medical and mental health reports on adoptive parents
    Home visit—all family members interviewed
    Home inspected

12. Assessment
    Three or four letters of reference required
    Social worker's general assessment of the family's ability to
        parent an adopted child

Other Selection Criteria

Some birthparents initially select the adoptive parents based on a
"gut feeling"; that is, a general sense of things being "right" or a feeling of "fate"—like it was just meant to be. Other birthparents have
very specific things they are looking for in parents for their child,
such as their religious beliefs, how they plan to discipline the child,
whether the child will be in child care, and so forth.

While it can be helpful to have a picture in your mind, we
encourage you to be open and flexible when considering parents. If
you have some absolutes that you would not change for anything,
then you should discuss those with your adoption counselor. However, it is important to let your counselor know the difference
between your "absolutes" and your "wish list."

SAMPLE CHECKLIST FOR SELECTING THE ADOPTING PARENTS

Absolute	Adoptive Parents Profile WISHLIST	MOST (1) TO LEAST (5) IMPORTANT				
		1	2	3	4	5
•	Married	x				
	Over the age of 30			x		
•	Some college education	x				
•	Financially stable		x			
•	Not particularly religious, spiritual beliefs are ok			x		
	Live in a rural or semi-rural environment				x	
•	Pro-choice, liberal politics, not racist, environmentalists	x				
	Enjoy and spend time in the outdoors		x			
	Involved with extended family		x			
•	Non-smokers	x				
•	Currently living in California or Oregon	x				

Age: Most adopting parents are in their 30s and 40s. This is commonly the age at which most couples discover, after trying to achieve a pregnancy (sometimes for 10 years or more!), that they will not be able to do so. Some adopting parents are in their twenties, though, and some are in their sixties. While age can tell you something about the person, it cannot be considered a predictor of the quality of the parenting. Good parenting comes at all ages!

Religion or Spiritual Beliefs: For some birthmothers, religion is very important. Often birthmothers will tell us, "I only want Christian couples" or "I am strongly against a religious home." When a birthmother asks us to present to her only those couples who consider themselves Christian, the category may include a wide range of beliefs and practices. Talk to your counselor about what you mean by "Christian" couples only. This will help your counselor include anyone she thinks might fit your criteria. It is better for you that she includes people you may not have originally considered than if she fails to give you information on someone you might have liked.

Couples With or Without Children: Sometimes birthmoms pick a couple because they do not have any other children. These mothers may want their child to be the first for several reasons: so the child will get undivided attention; because they believe the couple will be especially excited; or even because it seems more fair to pick a couple who has no children rather than one who has already experienced parenting. Other birthmothers find they are drawn to selecting a family who already has children for different reasons: they want to be sure their child will have a sibling; they can get a sense of how the couple parents by watching them with their other children; or they feel more comfortable placing a child with a family who already knows what parenting is all about. If the couple's other child is adopted, the birthmother can also see for herself how comfortable the family is with adoption or ongoing contact with a birth family.

Working Parents: It is difficult these days to find mothers or fathers who can afford to stay home with their children full time. Some adopting couples, however, have positioned themselves to take extended time off from work after an adoption, or they may be able to stop working altogether. Some parents have arranged for maternity or paternity leave along with sick and vacation time and others have jobs that are flexible enough to work around caring for a new baby.

If it is important to you that the family you choose does not use child care, tell your counselor to pre-select only those couples who have indicated to their adoption provider that this is their plan. Of course, you have no guarantees that their plans will not change sometime in the future.

Single Parents: We see more and more single men and women who decide to parent without waiting for a partner to come into their lives. Many of these men and women have extended families and a large, close circle of friends who will help them create the type of family they feel is important for raising a child. These "singles" can be very motivated and dedicated to the task of parenting.

Don't assume a single parent will not be a full-time parent to the child. Some single parents have either financial or family resources to help make it possible for them to stay home and raise the child. If this is the case, ask to meet and interview that person or family member.

In considering a single parent, the answers to some questions may carry much more significance. Will this child have relatives who accept and welcome him into the family? Who will care for the child if something were to happen to the parent? You should find out if the single parent has a strong network of family and friends who will support the adoption, openness, and ongoing contact.

Adoptive Parents with Disabilities: Prospective adoptive parents may have disabilities, just like the rest of us, sometimes visible, sometimes not. Disabilities can include obvious ones, like being blind, deaf or confined to a wheelchair, or disabilities like multiple sclerosis or chronic fatigue syndrome, which may not be as apparent. We have worked with parents with a range of disabilities who have successfully adopted babies. Sometimes they have made adaptations in their home or have had additional assistance with their newborn, but they have been loving and attentive parents. Having a disability does not prevent a person from being a great parent. In an open adoption, it is important to discuss the disability and the adoptive parents' plans for any necessary adjustments to their environment. If you choose an adoptive parent with a disability, your counselor can assist you with any questions or issues you may have, if you find that it is difficult to broach the subject of their parenting plans.

Gay-Lesbian Parenting: Many agencies and attorneys have profiles on gay and lesbian prospective adoptive parents. See Chapter 11 for more discussion on this topic.

Deciding to Meet the Prospective Parents

Most birthparents that meet the adoptive parents are glad they did. There is so much that does not show up on a questionnaire or a letter or a home study. By meeting the prospective parents, you can feel much more comfortable with your choice and your vision for the future. If you are undecided about meeting the family, a good intermediate step is to talk to them on the phone. This allows you to get a better idea of who they are without the commitment of meeting. If the call does not go well, and you decide they are not the right couple for you, you can let your counselor know and spare yourself and the family the emotional investment of a meeting. And if everything goes well on the phone, you will all be more comfortable with each other if you do decide to meet.

While most birthparents prefer to narrow their choice down to one couple to meet, and then move on to another couple if it does not work out, other birthparents feel the need to meet with two or maybe even three possible couples. While this may be necessary to find the parents that are right for you, it can also be an emotionally draining experience.

Meeting the Couple

You can choose to meet with the couple anywhere that feels comfortable for you—a park, a restaurant, your house, a school, your counselor's office, or maybe the adoption center office. You may choose to go to the adoptive family's home to meet, which can give you more information about them. These meetings can last for quite a while, up to three hours if they are going well. We highly recommend you ask your adoption counselor to accompany you to the meeting and help facilitate the discussion. She will undoubtedly have orchestrated many of these meetings before and can lend some structure and comfort to the meeting. You will also find it helpful to sort through your feelings and impressions after the meeting with the counselor.

As nervous as you are to meet the prospective adoptive parents for your child, they are more nervous! The first meeting is really about getting to know each other a little bit and seeing if there are enough commonalities so that you would feel comfortable committing to one another. Agreeing to meet is not a commitment to proceed with an adoption, or with that particular couple. Here are some tips for handling the meeting:

- Write your questions down
- Bring the birthfather or a supportive family member or friend
- Have your counselor meet the couple with you
- Set the ground rules ahead of time (for example, "Regardless of how our meeting goes, let's all take some time to think about whether we are ready to commit to one another.")
- Bring pictures of family, friends, the birthfather
- Review your Adoptive Parent Wish List before and after the meeting

SAMPLE QUESTIONS FOR YOU TO ASK THE
PROSPECTIVE PARENTS

- How long have you known each other? How did you meet?
- How long have you been married?
- Have either of you been married before? Any children? Do they live with you?
- Why do you want to adopt? What methods have you tried to become pregnant?
- Are you still trying to get pregnant?
- How do you plan to tell the child about being adopted?
- How do you feel about remaining in contact with me? With my family?
- What kind of contact are you envisioning?
- What are your religious beliefs and practices?
- What does your family think about adoption?
- How close are you to your family/relatives? How often do you see/spend time with them?
- Have you talked to your other child(ren) about a new baby? What was their reaction?
- Do you plan to have more children?
- What if you were to become pregnant? Would you still want to adopt my baby?
- What are your child-rearing beliefs and practices?
- If the child is another race than the parents, how do you envision living as a transracial family?
- Do you have any health or mental health problems in your history?
- Under what conditions would you decide you did not want to adopt my baby?
- Are you willing to help me with my pregnancy-related financial needs?
- What if my baby was born with a disability or health problem? Would you still want to adopt?

Bring a Support Person

It is helpful if you have a friend (the birthfather?) with you at this meeting for support. It can be intimidating if it's just you and the couple. If you bring a friend or family member who is supportive of your decision, and whose opinion you value, she can help you evaluate your feelings about the meeting afterward.

Sensitive Information

Discussing sensitive but necessary information is where a counselor can really help you. There may be topics which need to be talked about that are terribly difficult, for example, your or the adoptive parents' drug or alcohol use, mental health history, or HIV status. An adoption counselor is used to handling these uncomfortable discussions with sensitivity and care.

Starting Your Meeting

When you first meet, it will be a little awkward. One way to break the ice is to bring some pictures of your family and the birthfather (if possible), and ask the couple to bring pictures of their family, their home, and fun places they like to go. This allows you to know a little more about them in an informal way.

There is a tendency at these first meetings for a lot of the focus to be on you. It may be more natural for the couple to begin asking you, "So, when are you due? Have you had medical care? What does your family think? Do you know if it's a boy or a girl?" and so forth. Of course, you will want to talk to them about these issues, but you also want to make sure you find out about them. One approach we use is to have the adoptive parents start the meeting by talking about how they met each other. All couples like to reminisce about when they first fell in love, and so it is a comfortable (and sometimes funny) way to begin. It is then easier to ask them other questions, like why they want to adopt.

You can expect the prospective adoptive parents to come with a list of questions they want to ask you too. They probably didn't sleep a wink the night before, worrying about what you would think of them.

They probably worried about what to wear and are trying not to get their hopes up. They have undoubtedly suffered a lot of losses—unsuccessful conceptions, failed pregnancies, or perhaps an adoption attempt that didn't work out. Likewise, they are probably very excited. This may finally be their chance to be parents, after all this time. They are arriving to meet you with anxieties and fears and hopes and dreams. Just like you.

They will want to meet you and find out who you are, but they are also going to be concerned about the risks they may be taking in deciding to work with you. They will be concerned about the birthfather, especially if he is not going to be a part of the adoption planning. They will be worried about the health of the baby. They will wonder if they can trust you. Can they be sure you are serious about your decision? They will want to know everything about you, just like you will want to know everything about them. Be prepared to answer their questions openly and honestly.

QUESTIONS TO ANTICIPATE
FROM THE ADOPTING PARENTS

- When did you first learn you were pregnant?
- How did you come to the decision to place your child for adoption?
- Have you received counseling to help you determine if this is what you really want?
- Have you received prenatal care? How is your health? The baby's?
- What about the father of the baby? Does he know of your plans? Is he supportive?
- Do you want ongoing contact with us? How often? Visits? Phone calls? Letters?
- How does your family feel about your adoption plans? Do they want to meet us?
- What about drugs, alcohol, or smoking?
- Have you had an HIV test? Would you be willing to be tested?
- How sure are you about your adoption decision?
- What would cause you to change your mind about placing your baby for adoption? About placing your baby with us?

Is This the Right Couple for Me?

If you are like most birthmothers, you probably have a pretty good idea about the couple by the end of the meeting. Sometimes things just seem to click, and an hour into the meeting, you are talking as if you've known each other for a while. Other times, you may have an uneasy feeling during the meeting, a gut sense that things just aren't right. Talk to your counselor about how you felt about the couple, refer to your worksheet about the qualities you want in your child's new parents, ask yourself the following questions—and then follow your instincts. Don't settle for a situation that just doesn't seem right.

QUESTIONS TO ASK YOURSELF ABOUT THE PROSPECTIVE PARENTS

- Do I feel comfortable with them?
- Do I think I would be interested in developing a relationship with them?
- Do I think I could trust them?
- Do I feel they have respect for me?
- Are their ideas about ongoing contact close enough to what I want?
- Are they the type of parents I am looking for?
- Can I imagine handing them my baby?
- Can I imagine them being my baby's parents?

It's Your Decision

Even if you are pretty sure these are the right people, you should all agree, before you even begin the meeting, to give yourselves a day to think about it. Knowing you do not have to decide right away can help relieve some of the pressure of the day. Agree to call them or your adoption counselor within a day or two to confirm your decision.

After you have met with all of the prospective parents that interested you, the decision is now in your hands. Chances are, you already have a pretty good idea who the parents of your child will be.

Some birthmothers say they felt a tremendous relief when they found the adoptive parents for their child, like a burden was lifted from their shoulders. Other birthmothers agonized over the decision. It is often just a matter of your style in making decisions. Take your time, and do it according to your own timeline.

When You Cannot Find Adoptive Parents for Your Child

If you can't find parents for your child, and you have had the opportunity to select from a fair number of couples, it could be time to reevaluate your adoption plan. When a woman cannot find appropriate parents for her child, it could mean she is unsure of her decision. She may not be able to imagine anyone being a good enough parent, so she cannot let go and move forward.

Choosing adoption involves a great deal of letting go, not only of the child, but also of the ideal of "perfect parenting." After taking the responsibility of finding a family for the child, birthmoms should be able to say, "I've done the best I can with the best intentions." If you find that you just can't do that, adoption may not be right for you.

Understanding the Perspective of the Adopting Parents

Just like birthmothers, no two adopting parents or couples are alike. There are, however, common experiences adopting parents share which color the way they approach adoption. The most common link between adopting parents is their experience with infertility. The vast majority of prospective adoptive parents turn to adoption to build or complete their family because they themselves are unable to conceive or carry a pregnancy to term.

Infertility can have a number of different causes: dysfunction in the woman, in the man, in both partners, or as a result of the combination of the two individuals. The reason for their infertility may or may not be known. Sometimes infertility is treatable and sometimes not. Medicine has made great strides in helping couples achieve a successful pregnancy. Sometimes, though, the path to success is at great cost, emotionally and financially.

By the time a couple contacts an adoption organization, chances are they have spent a number of years trying to have a baby on their own. They may have been able to conceive a child but not carry it to term, resulting in miscarriages, or perhaps they have never been able to get pregnant at all. Whatever the reason, the process of attempting pregnancy over and over again, with monthly disappointments turning into yearly reminders, is very painful.

> *"I feel so damaged. I want to tell my husband that I will understand if he wants to marry someone else, so at least he can have children. I feel I should be able to give him the children that we always planned to have—that he wanted— but I just can't. I feel like a failure as a woman."*

Over hundreds of centuries, women have traditionally been the ones responsible for bearing, nurturing, and raising the children. Most women grow up assuming they will be mothers at some point, and they assume the decision will be theirs to make when the time is right. When a woman is unable to have children, the realization can be shocking, deeply shameful, and excruciatingly painful.

Agencies will help adoptive families explore their infertility history by talking with them about how long they tried to conceive, what approaches they have tried, how they made decisions to continue infertility treatments, and how they decided to stop pursuing medical treatments. Hopefully, adoptive parents are also prompted to explore their various losses, how they view adoption after their infertility experience, and how they feel about moving on. In some cases, agencies may recommend further counseling for the couple to help heal the wounds from their infertility experience and prepare them more fully for the adoption experience. The losses couples experience through infertility can significantly impact their readiness to adopt and affect the relationship they build with their child's birthfamily.

In the past, when babies were thought to be "blank slates" upon which the adoptive parents etched their values, traits, and history, it mattered less whether or not the couple had truly resolved its grief over the inability to have their own children. Birthmothers gave up their children and were never seen or heard from—then or in the future. With open adoption, this is not the case. Birthmothers and adopting parents meet and know each other. Many instances involve a lifetime relationship. This openness means the adoptive mother and father come face-to-face on a regular basis with the fact that they are not the biological parents of the child.

For some adoptive parents, openness can be very confusing and threatening. How can they truly feel like parents when there is this other parent they must meet and get to know? Will the birthmother ever go away and let them become the parents they have always wanted to be? Unless the adoptive parents have had some personal experience with adoption, have done a lot of reading, or have asked a lot of questions, they will not likely be sold on the openness idea at the outset. Even meeting a birthparent can feel threatening.

Many of the conflicts that surface during the course of your relationship with the couple have their roots in fear. Your fear is that the couple won't love your child or won't honor their word to allow you to be part of their lives after the adoption. Their fear is that you won't be able to let go of the baby and let them be the mommy and daddy. Most of these fears can be calmed and addressed through good communication. This is easier said than done, especially if you do not know each other very well. Each of you is treading lightly with the other, hoping not to offend or say the wrong thing. A counselor who is experienced in adoption can make a tremendous difference as you navigate the beginnings of your relationship.

F E A R S & F E E L I N G S

BIRTH PARENT

What if they don't like me?

Can I trust them to honor their word that they will continue to welcome me in their lives?

What if they don't like my child?

I feel so out of control. What if they change their mind? What if they don't want my baby?

I feel like they are getting everything out of this. I feel such loss.

I am so jealous of what they have. They have love, and a home and money and now they'll have my baby too.

The adopting mother doesn't really seem HAPPY. I'm afraid she might have changed her mind. What if my baby doesn't make her happy? I want at least one of us to be happy about this.

Everytime we talk, she makes it sound like parenting is so difficult. Is my baby a burden to them? Is my baby happy? It worries me.

I do want to see the baby, but I really miss the adopting couple too. I like seeing them with my baby. It really reassures me that they are the good parents I thought they were going to be, and that they still care about me. It makes me feel better about my decision.

ADOPTING PARENT

What if she doesn't like us?

Can we trust her to keep her word about the adoption?

What if she keeps acting like "mom"?

I feel like my whole life is dependent on the birth mother. I feel so out of control.

I feel like she has all the power. Whatever she says goes.

I am so jealous that I can't be the one to be pregnant. Why can't I be the one to give my husband a baby?

I'm afraid that if I'm too happy around the birthmother that she'll feel like I'm being insensitive to her loss, so I kind of keep my JOY to myself around her. It's hard though to contain my excitement!

When she calls and asks me how the baby is I find it hard to say how well we're doing and what a good baby she is. I'm afraid she'll think it sounds too fun and easy and she'll change her mind and want the baby back.

She wants to come visit. I get scared that she will see how adorable her baby is and want her back. Even sending pictures she asks for—sometimes I'm tempted to send the ones that aren't quite as cute. Isn't that terrible?

Chapter 4:
MOVING AHEAD WITH YOUR ADOPTION PLAN

While some birthparents begin to make their adoption plan in their first trimester, others wait until later in their pregnancy, until after they have actually given birth, or until after they have tried parenting for a while. There is no right or wrong time to decide on adoption, but there are some typical processes to go through mentally, emotionally, and legally.

Once you've made a decision about what kind of adoption best suits you, certain steps must be taken. These may include contacting an attorney or agency, beginning or continuing prenatal care, arranging some kind of health insurance, beginning the Interstate Compact (ICPC) process if you and the adoptive family live in different states, notifying the Bureau of Indian Affairs if you have Native American heritage, involving the birthfather legally, and so forth. The agency or attorney you choose to work with can advise you on the criteria that fit your particular situation and your specific state laws. It is also highly recommended that you include counseling in order to prepare emotionally for your adoption. Make sure the agency or attorney provides a counselor specializing in adoption who can help you navigate the emotional and logistical process of placing a child for adoption. Counseling should be offered, encouraged and free of charge to you.

Building a Relationship with the Adoptive Parents

One important step in preparing for an adoption is to begin building a relationship with the adoptive parents. Naturally, this relationship can take many forms, depending on the kind of openness you desire. Assuming that you have selected adoptive parents for your child, you can move on to the next step in growing more comfortable with the adoptive parents and with your decision.

The "Honeymoon Period"

Many birthparents speak of an initial "honeymoon period" with the parents they have chosen. If you live close enough, you may wish to spend time with them throughout your pregnancy in any number of ways. There may be people in your life—friends, family, and children, for example, who you would like the parents to meet. There may be people in their lives they would like you to meet. You may want to get together informally for a meal, an outing, or to see their home and community. It may be more reassuring when the time comes to say good-bye to your child if you already have a picture in your mind's eye of the house where the child will be living and the people who will love him. Or you may prefer much less contact; it really depends on your comfort level.

Sometimes adoptive parents want to accompany you to a doctor appointment or ultrasound. For most adoptive parents, this is their way of connecting to you and your baby. Going to a prenatal appointment, hearing the baby's heartbeat, or actually viewing the baby during an ultrasound may be the closest an infertile couple will come to participating in a pregnancy. This arrangement is your decision however and must be something you are completely comfortable with. This is *your* pregnancy, *your* body, and *your* baby until you say differently. It is up to you to decide how much of your pregnancy you want to share with others.

At this stage of your relationship with the couple, you may be wavering about the degree of closeness you want now and in the future with the adoptive parents, and eventually with the child. On the one hand, closeness enables you to feel connected. On the other hand, too much contact may feel invasive or burdensome, or it may complicate your final decision to place once the child is born. Although you do not have to decide this once and for all today, you may wish to give some thought as to what feels most appropriate to you. It is important to be able to set privacy boundaries when you feel the need.

"During my pregnancy, the adoptive mom and I got really close. We had a lot in common. The adoptive father felt like a big brother. I felt like they were part of my family."

"The adoptive mom and I called each other every other week, and we went to lunch a few times, but I felt kind of funny getting too close to them, so I decided to keep my distance. Actually, the father of the child was really the one who kept in touch with them."

"My relationship with the adoptive parents before the birth wasn't as close as it became after the birth. Before the birth, we only got together twice: once for our first meeting, and once for a barbecue at my parents' home."

If you and the adoptive parents are getting along well, you may be tempted to talk less regularly with your counselor, or you may feel that counseling is now less important. After all, who needs counseling when things are going well, right? Try to keep in mind that both positive and negative emotions are somewhat fleeting during a pregnancy and adoption placement. If you are not building a relationship with a counselor now, it will feel awkward to reach out to someone when your feelings become more painful.

Handling Disagreements

You can expect to have some disagreements with your adoptive couple. It is completely normal to experience conflict while you are building your relationship, and it can even have a positive impact in the long run. If you can get through a disagreement during the pregnancy, it will pave the way for better conflict resolution skills when the baby actually arrives and the emotional temperature escalates. It is very important that you are able to talk with the adoptive parents about things that really matter to you. If you find yourself biting your tongue for fear of saying something that may upset them, or if you feel you are avoiding some topic you know is important to discuss, ask your counselor for help approaching these delicate subjects. Hopefully, your adoptive parents will also have a counselor they can consult about their challenging feelings. If something is really bothering you about how things are progressing, the problem probably won't go away on its own and may just need some discussion to clear the air.

One of the most toxic elements of any match is the "walking on eggshells" syndrome, when the birth parent and/or the adoptive parents are tiptoeing around strong negative feelings. This bodes very poorly for the future of a healthy adoption. Maybe you or the adoptive parents come from a family where the direct and honest expression of feelings is not the norm.

It is very normal for the comfort you feel with the parents to ebb and flow. Toward the end of the pregnancy, you may even feel resentful or jealous as you begin to get in touch with the reality of losing your role as the mother. Give your feelings a lot of latitude through this adoption process. It's hard to predict exactly how you will feel, and having some compassion for yourself will help.

Creating an Adoption Agreement

Once you have established a relationship with your prospective adoptive parents, you can begin to work on an adoption agreement that will outline each of your wishes for contact, both before and after the birth. These agreements, called "open adoption agreements" or "cooperative adoption agreements" by adoption practitioners, can be a guide in defining your relationship but are not, in most states, legally binding. The climate in the adoption community, however, may be reversing. Many legislatures are drafting changes in adoption law that would include cooperative adoption agreements among the legal documents filed with an adoption. The sample questions below cover both pre- and post-birth contact and are a tool to develop your own agreement. Depending on your relationship and level of trust, the agreement can be very informal or very structured and detailed. (For a list of issues to consider during your hospital stay, see the "Hospital Checklist" in Chapter 6.)

SAMPLE QUESTIONS FOR AN ADOPTION AGREEMENT

Pre-Birth Contact

- Before the delivery, how often will we talk on the phone? How often will we visit?

- If we visit, where will the visits take place?

- Do my children or other family members want to meet or visit the adoptive parents?

- Do I want the adoptive parents to accompany me to my prenatal visits?

- When I am ready to go to the hospital and deliver, who will call the adoptive parents to inform them? Do I want them to come to the hospital right away or wait until after I deliver?

Post-Birth Contact

- After the birth, who will make the first contact, the adoptive parents or me? How soon after the birth will I want to talk to them or see them?

- During the first year, how often do I want letters and pictures sent to me?

- During the first year, how often do I want to visit? Will the visits take place at my house, the adoptive parents' house, or the counselor's office?

- If my children or other family members wish continued contact, what will the contact consist of and do the adoptive parents feel okay about this?

- How will the child's first birthday be celebrated?

- Do we want to exchange Mother's Day cards? (Some birthparents appreciate this gesture, while others find it unnecessary or unwelcome.)

- After the first year, how often do I want to receive letters and pictures? How often do I want to visit?

- If problems develop in our relationship, how will I resolve them? Are we both willing to seek counseling to resolve differences?

Sensitivity to the Adoptive Parents

Besides having compassion for yourself, the ability to empathize with the adoptive parents will be very helpful. Chances are, this is their first time going through an adoption, and they will be as anxious and unsure of the process as you are, if not more so! The media bombards adoptive parents with stories about "adoptions gone bad." Television shows featuring sensational stories often focus on birthparents who take their baby back or embezzle tens of thousands of dollars from unsuspecting couples. Your adoptive family's own friends and relatives may be questioning their decision to participate in an open adoption and may need education about its benefits. And remember, most people who choose to create their family through adoption have suffered infertility problems. This often involves years of invasive, unsuccessful, and financially draining procedures that strip people of their sense of control. The adoptive parents that you have chosen may be left with emotional vulnerabilities or wounds, perhaps feeling they were not meant to be parents or are not equipped to be good parents.

Your sensitivity to these issues will help the adoptive parents you choose feel "entitled" to be your child's parents. Communicating your understanding of their losses will go a long way toward establishing mutual respect and consideration. Reassuring the adoptive couple of your confidence in them may help with their fears about the process. An adoptive mom expresses these feelings in her own words:

"We waited so long and went through so much to adopt a baby, but when we were finally blessed with a child, I felt like a fraud. I felt like I was pretending to be a real parent, when I knew I wasn't. I felt the need to cover up the fact that

this child was not biologically ours. I also felt a great burden on my shoulders—I had to be the perfect parent. After all, I was entrusted with this child who was a miracle in my eyes; I had to be the perfect mother in return. It took me months to realize that becoming an adoptive mother was becoming a real parent, and that my child's differences from us were what made her so beautiful. I also finally realized that nobody is a perfect parent. We all just have the responsibility to try our hardest and be the best role models for our children. Looking back on this now, I wish our birthmother had in some way verbally given us her permission during the adoption process to parent her child. I wish she had said that she didn't expect perfection from us, just our very best."

Over the course of the match, it will be very helpful if both you and the adoptive couple can develop a sense of tolerance and acceptance for one another. Each of you will have idiosyncrasies that may seem foreign to the other. After being very selective in choosing the parents, and then working hard to resolve disagreements, acceptance of differences can be a healthy part of any long-term relationship.

What If We Live Far Away from Each Other?

When birthparents choose adoptive parents who live far away or in another state, an open adoption can still proceed, although both parties have to be creative in making sure the logistical and emotional issues are addressed. Before you commit to any couple, it is advisable to meet them in person. If you are flying to another state to meet a family, make it explicit that this is simply a "getting to know you" meeting, without any obligations. Most times, advance phone calls will help establish your relationship, but an actual face-to-face meeting is needed to address many of the sometimes-awkward topics necessary to make a final decision.

This may require one of you to travel to the other's hometown, but geographic distance should not prevent you from meeting and getting to know one another before the birth.

"We developed a great relationship in the four months before the birth. We talked on the phone a lot since they lived in Washington. Every month, the adoptive mom would come down and take me to the support group at the adoption agency. We would always have lunch together, and then we might shop for clothes."

Living with the Adoptive Parents

Some birthmothers, especially if they are young or single, choose to live with the adoptive parents through the remainder of their pregnancy. There are pros and cons to an arrangement like this. On the positive side, it will allow you to really get to know the family intimately. You can all prepare for the birth of the baby together, and if all goes well, you will feel very supported, loved, and nurtured by the family to whom you are entrusting your baby. However, this type of arrangement requires that people be quite flexible, as well as good communicators. This kind of closeness will most likely bring up conflict, and both the birthmother and the adoptive family will have to be committed to working through the difficulties that will naturally arise. Birthmothers have also reported that leaving the adoptive parents' home after the baby is born is especially difficult. Not only are they feeling the loss of their baby, but they are also experiencing a loss as the relationship with the adoptive parents changes. It can feel bittersweet to see the adoptive parents focusing so much on the new baby when they previously focused all their attention on you!

Many adoption professionals caution against this type of arrangement for another reason. They feel that by living with the adoptive family during your pregnancy, your sense of obligation to them will increase. This could heavily influence your freedom to choose to parent the baby after his or her birth because you might feel hesitant to do so after all they've done for you.

A Few Words about Counseling

Birthmothers and birthfathers come into the adoption process with varied opinions about counseling. Some have had very positive relationships with counselors; others have found counseling not helpful, or even harmful. Most people have never even talked with a counselor about personal issues. Regardless of your previous experience, it is strongly recommended that you have some kind of professional guidance through the often-tumultuous process of placing your child for adoption. There are many ups and downs as you navigate through the uncertainty of adoption, and having an advocate can be essential.

"I wish I had received more counseling when it was new and raw because I am so distanced now—I think I just stuffed my feelings."

How Can an Adoption Counselor Help You?

First of all, she can provide you with logistical and emotional information to help normalize your particular situation and prepare you for what is to come. She can advocate for you to ensure that you are creating the kind of adoption that fits for you. She can listen to your thoughts and feelings and provide support. For all of these reasons and more, it is especially important for you to feel comfortable with this person. Make sure it is a good fit!

Let your counselor know what you expect from counseling. Some birthmothers want a counselor to help guide them in making decisions, others simply want emotional support for the decisions they have already made, and still others really only need help moving from step to step.

Some agencies have separate counselors for the birthparents and the adoptive parents. However, if your counselor is also working with the adoptive parents, make sure you know what the limits of confidentiality are. Ask you counselor what guarantees you have that she will not divulge private information to the couple.

This would also be a good time to attend a birthparent support group, if there are any in your area, or to get the phone numbers of some other birthmothers who you can call for support. It can be extremely helpful to hear from other birthmothers as you decide what kind of adoption is best for you. Also, very few people in the world know what it is like to place a child for adoption. Hearing other birthmoms will reassure you that what you are experiencing is normal. Being able to talk to those that have been there can minimize the isolation you may feel.

Chapter 5:
YOUR PREGNANCY

"I felt overwhelmed and lonely."

"Depressed, stressed, in denial, scared, and betrayed, but also happy in a way."

"Excited!"

"I hardly had time to experience my pregnancy. I felt like my life was so screwed up."

"I was in shock. I felt very upset and worried because I didn't find out that I was pregnant until I was about eight months along. I was going through mass confusion and trying to figure out how to break the news to everyone and handle the rejection I would get in return."

The above are all actual feelings women have expressed to us upon discovering an unplanned pregnancy. Although many women acknowledge their pregnancies very early on and begin to think about their options, other women experience denial or detachment for many months. Some fear that if they admit they are pregnant, they will then have to do something about it. Others are trying to protect themselves from the emotional pain they feel is inevitable. As you eventually allow yourself to face your predicament, there will come a point when you have to make some decisions about your pregnancy.

Your Body and Your Pregnancy

Although each pregnancy is unique, there are physical signs that a lot of women will experience, such as morning sickness and tender breasts. You may also continue to have some kind of a period even after becoming pregnant. On the other hand, missing a menstrual cycle does not necessarily mean that you are pregnant. If you are worried and wonder if you are in fact pregnant, a pregnancy test can answer your question, and the earlier you find out, the better for you and your baby. You can do a home pregnancy test or go to a local pregnancy clinic for a free or low-cost confidential test. If you are afraid to do this alone, ask a friend or relative to accompany you. You may need support once you get the results, or you may already know the answer instinctively. "It took three tests and my trying to convince the doctors that I knew I was pregnant before the tests came back positive," one woman told us.

If you find out you are pregnant, you have lots of decisions to make. **Take it slowly.** There is no need at this point to rush into a decision, no matter how far along you are. Take time to absorb the fact and experience all the emotions that will most likely occur, such as shock, fear, happiness, anger, or relief.

As your pregnancy progresses, the physical signs and symptoms will become apparent. You may feel slow, sluggish, tired, or grumpy. You may be worried because your jeans no longer fit, or fear that your boyfriend no longer finds you attractive. You may be very scared your parents will figure out that all the big shirts and second helpings aren't just a phase you're going through. (Some young women we have worked with lived at home through their entire pregnancy without their parents suspecting a thing. We call this the "elephant in the living room" syndrome.)

At other times, you may love being pregnant. You find you are getting lots of attention and people around you are kinder and more considerate. Strangers smile and wish you well. Your pregnancy will undoubtedly bring up a multitude of feelings for you, ranging from joy to despair.

"I had a great pregnancy. I was so excited about the baby and the whole idea of being pregnant. I enjoyed the ultrasound and found out it was going to be a boy. One of the neatest parts was lying in bed at night and watching him

move around in my stomach. It was a very positive experience."

Fear and Expectations

"If I love my baby now, will I ever be able to let her go?" You will ask yourself this question many times during your pregnancy if you have decided on adoption. You may try to remain detached as you go through your pregnancy because you think it will be easier when the time comes to place your baby with the adoptive parents. However, as much as you want to stay detached, you ARE bonded with your baby. You are caring for and loving your baby while you are pregnant. Maybe it's not a conscious attachment, but you may wake up one day with an overpowering love for the baby you are carrying. This may happen the first time you feel your baby kick, or when you see your first ultrasound. Even if you never thought you wanted to be a mom, it is difficult not to feel love for your baby. Bonding with your baby does not mean you cannot place her for adoption, nor does it prevent the adoptive parents from bonding with the baby after the birth and placement.

You may be afraid to show how excited or content you are in front of the adoptive parents, your parents, or your partner because you are worried they might think you are changing your mind about the adoption. Allowing yourself to feel happy or sad or fearful or content doesn't need to disrupt your adoption plan. The feelings are part of the normal range for all pregnant women, and to some extent, you will feel these things whether you parent your baby or place her for adoption.

> *"I pretty much ignored the pregnancy. I didn't realize it would be the only one I would ever have, so I stayed away from learning anything about it. I just let it happen. I always loved the baby, but I knew I would place her for adoption. But I loved playing with her while I carried her."*

"It's a Girl!"

You may have decided to place your baby for adoption before finding out the gender. Although ultrasounds are not one hundred percent effective in establishing gender, they are usually accurate, and most women today have an ultrasound sometime during their pregnancy. You may also have an amniocentesis if your doctor recommends it, which will identify the baby's gender. The news that your baby is a boy or a girl can alter your feelings about the placement, momentarily or permanently. You may already have all boys, and upon finding out the baby is a girl, you can't imagine giving up the chance to raise a daughter. Or maybe you believe boys are easier to raise than girls. Perhaps the birthfather learns he will be the father of a son, and all of a sudden, the baby is a reality to him, and he doesn't agree with the adoption anymore. Finding out the baby's gender can make the child more real. Take time to explore your feelings about parenting or placing a baby boy or baby girl to see if the gender of the baby will impact your decision.

"Twins (or More)!"

Finding out you are pregnant with twins may complicate your adoption decision. Although caring for twins is more difficult than caring for one baby, there can be an emotional pull toward parenting twins. While most adoptive parents would be thrilled at the opportunity to parent two babies, some may need time to decide if they want to adopt more than one child. Many cities have resources for the parents of twins, and you can ask your medical practitioner or counselor for a referral to these organizations. They might be able to put you in touch with other parents of twins you can talk to about the reality of having two babies.

Traumatic Situations and Their Effect on Adoption Placement

Some women's pregnancies are the result of incest or rape. Some women are battered while pregnant. In addition to dealing with an unwanted pregnancy, these women are also dealing with overwhelming feelings of rage, resentment, fear, and guilt. If you are in this situation, it is essential that you seek help from professionals who are experts in dealing with violence against women. Phone books have listings you can call for assistance. You may decide to carry the pregnancy to term but still have a lot of mixed feelings about the pregnancy and the baby. Some of your anger toward the perpetrator may get confused with your feelings for your baby, even though you can intellectually distinguish between the person who caused you harm and your unborn child.

In instances like these, it is sometimes hard to ask for and receive the support you need. Some people may blame you or not believe you. Remember that you are dealing with two crises at once, which is an overload for anyone. It is imperative that you muster up as much support for yourself as possible. Seek out people who are non-judgmental and caring. You may need help talking with the prospective adoptive parents about the circumstances surrounding your pregnancy, and this is a very important time to have a counselor or support person available.

Preparing for the Delivery

"Before the birth, I felt guilty because I couldn't give my little girl the things she needed to be healthy and happy once she was born. It was difficult preparing myself for the birth and eventual relinquishment of my rights. I loved my baby from the time I learned I was pregnant. It was because I loved her so much that I was able to consider adoption in the first place."

As your pregnancy progresses, you will start thinking about childbirth. If this is your first pregnancy, the unknown aspects of actually giving birth can be scary. You may have lots of fears and apprehensions about delivering a baby, especially when you begin to hear other women's horror stories of labor and delivery. The following are some choices you can make during this time to help alleviate some of your fears.

Medical Insurance and Prenatal Care: Many women delay seeking medical care until late in their pregnancies because they do not have medical insurance. If you are not covered by an insurance plan, either through your parents or your own employment, you may be eligible for medical coverage through a state-sponsored program. Call or visit your local social service office and ask about the Medicaid program. You may qualify for coverage of your pregnancy-related medical care, even if you are employed or are a minor living at home and have no other coverage. You can make your inquiries confidentially.

If you are employed and covered through your work, check your company's current health plan. If you are covered by your parents' health plan and don't want them to know just yet about your pregnancy, you can make a confidential appointment for your care. Check with an insurance company representative to find out if your parents will receive any correspondence related to your care.

Another option for medical coverage is to ask the adoptive parents to assist with medical expenses, if this is legal in your state. Check with your attorney or an adoption agency if you are not sure. Although this is a legally allowable expense in most states, there are additional issues to consider if you are asking the adoptive parents to help with medical expenses. First and foremost, you should think about how this would impact your relationship with the adoptive parents. Whenever large sums of money are involved in an adoptive relationship, it "ups the ante," so to speak, and can be the source of conflict and misunderstanding. For example, will you feel more obliged to place your baby with the adoptive parents if they are paying your medical bills, even though you may change your mind? Will the adoptive parents feel they have the right to call your doctor for updates on your health care and be present for your prenatal visits if they are funding this expense?

If you and the adoptive parents agree on this expense, make sure you are both very clear about expectations and involvement during your pregnancy. Pregnancy-related expenses are considered a gift in most states. If the adoptive parents pay for this expense, and then you decide to parent, the financial loss to them can be quite exorbitant. Additionally, you may feel terribly guilty about changing your mind and causing them financial hardship.

Your counselor or attorney can help you and the adoptive parents work out a clear agreement about medical expenses and mediate if there are misunderstandings. Be sure to have someone available to help with this before you accept any money for medical care. In some states, you may be required to fill out financial request forms before any money is exchanged.

Some of the best hospitals and medical practitioners we work with accept government-funded health insurance (Medicaid). Many of these doctors and hospitals offer support and guidance to women choosing adoption, during both the pregnancy and the difficult postpartum period. The doctors, nurses, midwives, and social workers in hospitals are, for the most part, extremely supportive of adoption and are willing to work with birthparents and adoptive parents to implement their wishes. Of course, there are exceptions. On occasion, there are some medical personnel who, for personal reasons, are unsupportive and even judgmental. Try to remember that any unsupportive comment is completely unprofessional and more a reflection of their personal views than your adoption decision. If you are offended by the words of your healthcare practitioner, ask for someone else to work with you. If you do not know where to start looking for health care, here are some tips:

- Look in the phone book for your local health clinic or public hospital. Ask if you need to have insurance before a prenatal visit. Many public hospitals have financial offices where you can fill out your eligibility paperwork and social workers who can help you walk through the process.
- If you have private insurance but do not have an OB/GYN, ask for a list of doctors affiliated with your health plan. Private health plans have the names of doctors who accept new patients, often based on due dates. The later in your pregnancy, the more limited your choice of a health care practitioner may be.
- Many large Health Maintenance Organizations (HMOs) will set up your first prenatal visit if you call your local hospital or clinic. You may need to be a member, although some HMOs accept Medicaid as payment. You will be assigned a doctor or nurse practitioner.
- Ask friends, relatives, or co-workers if they can recommend a doctor who accepts the type of insurance you have.
- If you have selected adoptive parents, ask them to help you find a doctor or midwife. Most adoptive parents have been through a maze of medical experiences and are very savvy about the medical system, which can seem intimidating. Most adoptive parents are happy to assist.
- Ask your counselor, your adoption social worker, or your attorney for referrals or assistance in finding good, supportive, high-quality medical care. They probably have some very good information and personal knowledge about doctors, insurance, and how to find the very best medical care available.

Childbirth Preparation Classes: You may want to know as much as possible about the birthing process so you will be prepared and participate to the fullest extent possible in your labor and delivery. Most hospitals offer childbirth preparation classes or will give you information about where you can find a class. You may also want to ask your adoption counselor if they can recommend a private childbirth educator or a video on childbirth. Childbirth education classes can be an excellent way to prepare yourself for your delivery, but they are generally full of excited couples who are anticipating parenting, and this type of setting may feel uncomfortable.

A private childbirth educator can offer information and support in a cozy setting, and you can include your support people in the class. You can also hire a doula who can support you through your labor and delivery. You should also decide if you want the adoptive parents to participate in the classes with you, and whether or not you actually want them to be at the hospital during the labor and delivery. Many adoptive parents are delighted to be involved. This is also the time to begin thinking about who your coach will be during labor. Will it be your partner? A friend? A relative? The adoptive parents? You need a support person who can totally focus on you and your needs during your labor.

Prenatal Visits: If you have chosen the adoptive parents before your delivery, you may want to involve them in your prenatal care. Some birthmothers are comfortable with this and enjoy having the adoptive parents accompany them to their doctor appointments, while others feel it is a very private and personal experience. Either way is okay, but it needs to be totally your choice. Adoptive parents are often anxious about your prenatal care and the health of the baby, but it is not appropriate for them to accompany you to your doctor visits without being invited or to contact your doctor without your permission. In addition to getting good physical care during this time, you need understanding and a health care practitioner who can support you and your decisions fully.

Drugs, Alcohol, and Cigarettes: If you have used drugs, alcohol, or cigarettes during your pregnancy, you must talk to your health care practitioner about your usage, as difficult as that may be. This is a health-related issue, and your doctor will make treatment recommendations that she thinks are appropriate. Not only is it important to consult with your adoption counselor about informing the adoptive couple of your baby's exposure to alcohol or drugs, but you may also need your counselor's help in alerting the hospital so the personnel on staff may adequately prepare. Most hospitals these days will test any baby for drugs if they suspect the mother of drug use. Some hospitals even have a policy of testing all newborns whose mothers have not had prenatal care or whose babies are being placed for adoption. If your baby tests positive for drugs at the hospital, the hospital staff may be obligated to report this to child welfare. Most hospitals will not interfere if they know that an adoption plan is being made for the child and that the adopting couple knew in advance about the possibility of drug exposure. * See CHART on next page.

Breast-feeding Plans: Although it is somewhat uncommon, some birthmothers do breast-feed, even though they are making an adoption plan. You may fear that if you breast-feed, you will not be able to part with your baby when it is time to place him or her for adoption. Or you may fear the reaction of others, especially your family or the adoptive parents. Birthmothers who do breast-feed do so for a number of reasons: to have a period of closeness with the baby, for the health and nutritional advantage, or just because it is a unique and wonderful experience. If you make this choice, it is helpful to discuss it beforehand with the adoptive parents and your health care practitioner. That way, everyone's expectations will be clear, and hopefully there will not be any negative reactions or pressure after the birth. Some adoptive moms are also interested in breast-feeding (Yes! It can really happen!) which can be a nice transition for your baby.

Alternative Birth Plan: You may decide you want to deliver at home, use a midwife instead of a doctor for your delivery, or deliver in an alternative birthing center (ABC) instead of a regular delivery room. If you are interested in exploring alternative birthing options and plans, there are lots of books available. Your local pregnancy clinic may have some names of midwives that assist in home births or hospital deliveries. In some states, however, certain insurance companies or Medicaid will not pay for a home delivery or a midwife, so make sure to know all of your resources before making a definite plan.

Effects of Alcohol, Tobacco and Other Drugs on Developing Babies

(note: table includes *some, but not all* of the effects)

Alcohol	Tobacco	Marijuana	Cocaine	Heroin
low birthweight below normal length smaller head and chest circumference	smaller infants low APGAR score shorter than normal	increased tremulousness altered vision response patterns	adverse growth effects low birthweight smaller head	low birthweight brain hemorrhages respiratory distress
increased risk for infants: early death respiratory difficulty feeding problems serious infections long term developmental problems		persisting tremors and startles	jitteriness cries shrilly	
		affects sleep arousal patterns	central nervous system irritability impaired ability to orient and to control muscles	
may show signs of alcohol withdrawal: tremors abnormal muscle tension			possible increase of crib death	

Excerpted with permission, from *Summary of Effects of Alcohol, Tobacco and Other Drugs on Developing Babies and Children* by the Prevention and Student Services Dept., Sacramento County Office of Education, 9738 Lincoln Village Drive, Sacramento CA 95827

Family, Friends, and You

"My family was very supportive, and I could always talk to them about anything. The counseling I received was valuable. My boyfriend was a wonderful support and was behind me every step of the way."

"They respected my decision, but I think they thought I would never go through with it. My father still hasn't forgiven my boyfriend or my mother for not trying to talk me out of it."

"My mother was always there for me when I needed to talk or a shoulder to cry on. I wouldn't have made it without her."

Almost everyone in your life who knows about your pregnancy and adoption plan will have a reaction, an opinion, or advice. Some of this may be helpful, some distressing. You should think about soliciting help from those people who offer you unconditional support during this time.

The quality of the relationship with your family members will probably have a lot to do with whether or not you confide in them. Many times, parents will react with disbelief, then anger, followed by understanding and support when the shock wears off. Some family members will never support your decision and will in fact make the pregnancy and adoption process even more difficult by sabotaging your efforts. If you cannot talk to your parents, try confiding in a sibling or close relative first. Again, try to pick someone who will support your decision, whether or not they would make the same decision if they were in your shoes.

Your decision to place your child for adoption is a personal and confidential matter, and in most states, you will not need your parents' permission to proceed. Consult with an attorney or your adoption counselor if you have any questions about laws pertaining to parental involvement.

"Neither of my parents or any of my family knew I was pregnant. They found out the day my son was born. They were in shock!"

"My friends really came through for me!"

Your friends can be the most important source of comfort and support, especially if your family or the birthfather is uninvolved or unsupportive. Having a good friend to talk to, someone to laugh and cry with, may be the most valuable support you have. Be willing to tell your friends what you need, and they will most likely be there with a shoulder and a hug.

Talking with Your Children about Your Pregnancy and Adoption Plan

"Sam, my oldest, still remembers and talks about Jeff. I think my family and I have reinforced that by telling him stories about Jeff and the adoption—he was so little at the time. I plan to tell Nathan when he is older, too."

If you have children, whether they live with you or not, you will probably struggle with how and when to tell them about your pregnancy and adoption plan. Some of the most frequent questions we get from birthparents involve talking to their children. Most kids, even very young ones, can sense that "something's up." One young mother, who hadn't yet discussed her pregnancy with her children, recalls admonishing her son and saying he was a nuisance. He replied, "Mothers who don't tell their children that they're pregnant are a nuisance!"

Kids react differently, depending on their age, developmental stage, and temperament. Young children need lots of reassurance and concrete explanations. They are often worried about themselves and their place in your family and may fantasize that if you give up this baby, you might "give them away, too." Use clear language, and don't be afraid to use the word adoption so that it will be a normal part of your young child's vocabulary. Saying things like, "Baby Justin went away" or "Suzanne isn't going to live with us right now" will only confuse your child, who may wonder where baby Justin went exactly or when Suzanne will live with you again.

It is important to stress the fact that, "although baby Heather will live with Bill and Cindy, you will always be my little girl and live with me." Storybooks about adoption with pictures can be a big help.

Ask your local librarian or call a bookstore in your area. Younger children often benefit from seeing the adoptive family's home so they have a picture in their mind's eye about where the baby will live. Picturing the baby in his or her room is reassuring and helps dispel the fantasy that the baby has just disappeared into thin air. A young mother describes how she involved her daughter in the adoption:

"I had a three-year-old daughter at the time of the placement. She got to meet the adoptive parents as well. She misses them a lot. She asks about her birthsister, and we look at pictures together. Every once in a while, she tells me that she wants her sister to come home. I explain that she lives with her parents now and not in Mommy's tummy anymore. She seems to accept this for now. The pictures do help a lot, though, and the fact that she knows where her birthsister lives."

Older children may want to be involved in the process and may ask if they can still visit their birthbrother or -sister. If you know the adoptive parents, including your kids in the relationship may ease some of your children's fears. We have included school-aged children in some of the counseling sessions, especially when discussing ongoing contact. Some of these kids decide on their own that they would like to send cards or pictures to their birthsibling. Discuss your child's concerns and wishes with the adoptive parents before the birth, if possible, so that you can agree on an acceptable level of contact between them and your children. Many adoptive parents are very open to ongoing visits, while others are uncomfortable with the idea.

If the adoptive parents have other children, biological or adopted, they may wonder about the impact of ongoing contact on their other children. Some families struggle with openness when they have more than one adopted child and one child's birthfamily is more involved than the other child's. If you are going to have a greater level of involvement than another birthparent, discuss with the adoptive family how this will affect all of the children involved. Some birthparents we have worked with generously included the child whose birthparents did not call or visit.

Even though your baby is placed for adoption, your children may still consider the child their brother or sister. A relationship exists and needs recognition. One birthmother describes her five-year-old daughter's reaction to the adoption of her younger sister:

"My daughter knows she has a birthsister and talks openly about it. They have a special relationship. They are full siblings, and we want them to know each other. My daughter seems to accept the adoption. We are committed to keeping their connection intact."

Children take their cues from the adults in their lives who they know and trust. If the grown-ups are relaxed and confident about the nature of the open adoption arrangements, their comfort goes a long way towards reassuring the children that relationships in their family are healthy. Regardless, placing a baby for adoption will be a significant loss for your child, and she will grieve. Give her a wide latitude to express her various feelings. Even though it will be difficult to see your child in pain, expressing anger and sorrow may be a normal part of your child's grieving process. Involving your child in counseling before and after the placement can be enormously helpful and can alleviate some of the burden you may feel from having to be your child's main support while you yourself are grieving. Talking to other birthparents that have children is another good way to understand and support your kids, and you might not feel so alone. We know some birthmoms who have regular get-togethers with other birthmothers and their children and have formed lasting relationships.

If you are worried that your child is unusually depressed, lethargic, or anxious, you should seek professional help immediately. A therapist can assess if your child is in need of further treatment. Most kids will have some emotional reaction, which is normal during times of stress and transition. It is common for them to feel sad and to exhibit some behavioral changes. However, if these behaviors seem extreme to you, do not hesitate to get professional help.

SOME COMMON REACTIONS FROM CHILDREN

- Curiosity (asking lots of questions)
- A regression in skills (such as toileting or eating independently)
- Anger or acting out
- Clinginess
- Acting overly protective of you
- Fearfulness (if you leave, will you return?)
- Apathy (lack of response or reaction)
- Withdrawal or silence
- Sadness
- Unwillingness at times to talk about the baby, the adoptive parents, or adoption in general

Other Adoption Issues

If you are an adoptee, this baby may have special significance for you, as he or she may be the first person you know to whom you are biologically related. While adoptees represent only a small percentage of the population in general, adoptees are overly represented in the birthmother population. It can be a very powerful experience to see your baby for the first time because your baby may resemble you in ways no one else in your family does. You may be especially surprised and overwhelmed by the feelings you have after the birth. This is true for all birthmothers, but we have been told by birthmoms who are also adoptees that the intensity is quite strong. Take some time in preparation for your delivery to explore and express your experience as an adoptee with a counselor, if possible.

If this is your second or third adoption, you may think it will not be as difficult this time. Some birthmoms we have worked with said their second placement was easier because they knew what to expect. Others told us it was much more difficult, perhaps because it revisited the grief from the first adoption or because they felt bad about another unplanned pregnancy. Losses are often complicated by other losses. They are not necessarily something we get good at handling just because we have experienced a lot of them. If you are considering a second placement, take time to examine the feelings surrounding your first adoption.

Saying Good-Bye—Grief Preparation

"No one is ever prepared. It was so hard!"

"I feel I was pretty prepared for the grieving process. I think I knew what to expect."

"I never knew I could hurt so much. I never thought I would cry so long."

Thinking about saying good-bye to your baby is a hard thing to do, so hard, in fact, that many women choose not to think about it at all while they are pregnant. Even if you are choosing an open adoption, and you will see your baby after the birth and placement, you will no longer be parenting your baby. In addition to planning an adoption for your baby, you are also giving up your role as a mother, a role that is almost sacred in our society. There is no way to completely prepare yourself for the grieving process, and there is no way to completely avoid the grief that comes after the delivery. There are some things, however, that you can do to help yourself through the difficult period after the birth:

- Write yourself a letter while you are pregnant and tell yourself why you are making this choice.
- Ask a friend or family member to stay with you after you deliver and talk openly and freely about what you are feeling.
- Keep a journal during your pregnancy and after your delivery.
- Plan some ways to pamper yourself.
- Write a letter to your baby during your pregnancy and postpartum period, describing what you are feeling and thinking.
- Try to hook up with a "Birthmother Buddy"—someone who has already placed a child for adoption.

Chapter 6:
HOSPITAL AND BIRTH

"My hospital experience was very positive. I had my own room for labor and delivery, which was very helpful. The nurses were really good to me and made me feel comfortable. All of the nurses and my doctor knew of my decision and respected my wishes. It was important to me that my delivery room could accommodate a big group. When my son was born, there was a full house. My stepmother was my labor coach, along with my boyfriend, who I met when I was three months pregnant. My father was holding my hand. The adoptive parents and their daughter were in the delivery room, too. And lastly, the doctor and nurses. It was a wonderful experience for all of us, as well as a very bonding time. I wouldn't change anything about my hospital experience."

"I wish I hadn't played 'ostrich' throughout my pregnancy."

"It was short and scary!"

Some women wait until the last minute and make no plans at all, while others have very detailed and specific ideas about their birthing experience. The choices about labor and delivery are yours, even if you are planning an adoption. The dark ages of adoption when women were drugged and their babies whisked away after the delivery, are thankfully gone. Today, most hospitals and their staff have experienced some form of open adoption, where the adoptive parents are part of the hospital experience.

Meeting with the Adoptive Parents before the Birth

It is a good idea to write up an agreement in regards to your plans for the hospital with the adoptive parents before you deliver, since there are many issues to discuss. While written agreements are not legally binding in most states, they can serve as a helpful tool to clarify your preferences regarding the hospital plan. Discussing your expectations can also reveal areas of conflict. Like any relationship, there is bound to be some disagreement between you and the adoptive parents. Conflict is not necessarily negative. The way you are able to work through and resolve disputes before the baby comes can be a testament to the strength of your relationship. Are the adoptive parents sensitive to your needs and feelings? Are you aware of their concerns and wishes? For many adoptive parents, your delivery will be as close as they will ever come to experiencing a birth, and some of their requests for the hospital stay may have to do with their own sadness about their infertility. The following checklist can be a guide for developing an agreement with the adoptive parents.

HOSPITAL CHECKLIST

- Do you want a natural delivery, or do you think you will want medication? (entirely your decision)
- Who will be at your labor? At your delivery? (Some hospitals restrict the number of people who can be in your room)
- Are you planning to breast-feed?
- Do you want your baby to room-in with you?
- Do you want to spend time alone with your baby?
- Do you want the adoptive parents to spend time alone with the baby?
- Do you want the baby to stay in the nursery but brought to your room when you want to see her?
- Who will hold the baby first?
- Who will do the feeding and caretaking of the baby? You? The adoptive parents? Or will you share this together?
- If your baby is a boy, will he be circumcised?
- How will the discharge from the hospital be handled? Will you leave before your baby is discharged? After? At the same time as the adoptive parents?

- What name will you put on the original birth certificate? (You will be asked to name the baby on his or her original birth certificate).

Informing the Hospital

Once you have made some decisions about your labor and delivery, it is a good idea to let the hospital know about your plans. You can send a letter to inform the hospital social worker or head nurse that you are planning an adoption and to introduce the adoptive parents. Your counselor or attorney can draft a letter to the hospital for you. The letter should include releases of information, allowing the hospital staff to disclose information about the labor and delivery to the adoptive parents, as well as to your counselor and attorney (if you wish information to be disclosed). It is additionally helpful to include information about the prospective adoptive parents, as well as their picture. Put a copy of the letter with your hospital luggage in case it isn't received by the hospital in time or is filed away in a locked office during the time you deliver.

Before your due date, you can arrange a tour of the hospital with your coach and the adoptive parents, if they are going to be there for your labor. This is a great opportunity to meet the social worker or head nurse; visit the labor, delivery, and postpartum rooms; see the nursery; and check out the parking, cafeteria, and waiting rooms. You can also ask if the hospital has previously worked with an adoption and find out if there are any restrictions or limitations.

SAMPLE QUESTIONS FOR THE HOSPITAL STAFF

- Have you previously handled open adoptions at your hospital?
- Do you restrict the number of people allowed in the labor and delivery room? If so, how many people are allowed?
- Do you have alternative birthing rooms, and if so, are there any requirements for using them?
- Can I have a private room?
- Are there any visiting restrictions for the adoptive parents or my family? If so, what are they?
- Do you allow cameras or camcorders in the labor and delivery area?

- If my baby stays in the nursery, can the adoptive parents visit whenever they like? Are there any restrictions?
- What paperwork will I have to sign in order for my baby to be released to the adoptive parents?
- How long can I stay in the hospital if I have no complications?
- What is the hospital discharge policy if the baby is ready to leave the hospital before I am, or vice versa?

Packing Your Bags

Babies come when *they* are ready, not necessarily when we are. So, while you may deliver "on time," you may also be weeks early or weeks late. Before you leave for the hospital, you might want to remember the following:

- Pack some comfortable, loose-fitting clothes.
- Besides essentials like toothbrush or deodorant, pack some lotion, perfume, lipstick, a chocolate bar—something that will make *you* feel good after the birth.
- Bring a soothing tape or a picture to focus on during labor.
- You may want to bring a baby outfit or toy to send home with the adoptive parents.
- Don't forget the camera (a small disposable is good if you don't have one).
- Bring a copy of your hospital letter.

Labor and Delivery

"My baby ended up being born three weeks late, and I started labor the morning I was induced. There was a wonderful nurse who spent most of the night just visiting with me before she had to go off duty. She left before the baby was born, but I had shared with her that the one thing I really wanted was a Butterfinger. When I went back to my room

after the delivery, I found one on the table next to my bed. I was able to spend three days with my little girl before giving her to the adoptive parents. It was great."

The actual birth of your baby will be a miraculous event, and maybe very different from what you expected. Your education and preparations will help you during this time, but don't be afraid to make a change of plans. Having a coach or someone else designated to relay your wishes could be critical to the comfort of your delivery. Even though you originally planned to have friends, family, and/or the adoptive parents at your bedside, you may decide to ask people to leave. You may end up having an unplanned cesarean section and not be able to use your Lamaze training. You might request an epidural because the pain is greater than you anticipated. You might have a very short labor and deliver before the adoptive parents or your support people can make it to the hospital (especially if they are coming from a distance), or you might be in labor for a very long time. Being prepared for any situation will ease your disappointment if your labor isn't exactly what you hoped for.

"I was dead tired from being in labor all night without sleep, I was alone, I had no idea what to expect, and I HURT!"

"I had a long labor, but after I received my epidural block, I had no pain and delivered my daughter with no problems. I was awestruck by the whole ordeal; I didn't talk much and watched everything with very large eyes. It was much less terrifying than I was expecting it all to be."

Over the years, we have seen some women deliver way past their official due date. We don't know if this is the result of inaccurate due dates or of birthmoms who aren't ready to let go of their babies. One birthmother described her birth and the letting-go process:

"When I was dilated to seven or eight, I started closing back up again. My midwife told me it was my way of not letting go. I had to go into the shower and actually say good-bye and let myself grieve before my baby could even be born physically."

What If My Baby Has a Problem?

Most deliveries are difficult but uncomplicated, or "normal," meaning the baby and the mother have no serious medical complications. A small percentage of births, however, result in serious problems for the mother and/or the baby. In these very difficult situations, the most critical issue is the health and safety of the mother and baby. Everyone's energy needs to be focused on this until both are medically stable. If the baby is born with serious medical problems or a genetic defect, you may all need to reassess your plans. It is critical to discuss the issue of a handicap prior to the delivery. The scope of the problem or handicap may not be immediately clear if, for instance, the baby has a breathing or respiratory problem, while other problems, such as Down's syndrome or a cleft palate, may be more identifiable. You and the adoptive parents will need to regroup and discuss your options after you have recovered from the delivery.

While some adoptive parents will make a commitment to adopt your baby no matter what the circumstances, many are reluctant to adopt a severely handicapped baby. Besides the medical issues, it is an enormously emotional subject. If the adoptive parents do choose to back out of an adoption, you will be left with many decisions. For example, will you parent the baby yourself, or will you search for other adoptive parents? You may be wounded by the adoptive parents' decision and too distraught to decide immediately. There are some agencies that specialize in special-needs adoptions, and your counselor can assist you in locating resources. You may be able to put your baby in foster care if you need some time to decide what to do. Although you will probably be exhausted and extremely stressed, it is important to ask for help during this time. It is also important for you to take all the time you need to assemble your support team and to consider all your options.

If your baby has medical problems and needs to remain in the hospital after your discharge, and if the adoptive parents are still committed to the adoption, you need to plan for care and visiting arrangements. Leaving an ill baby in the hospital may complicate any feelings of guilt and bewilderment you have. If you remain in close contact with your baby, you may decide to reconsider your adoption decision because you feel you are abandoning her when she needs you the most. You may also feel you somehow caused the problem that resulted in your child's medical condition. Your counselor is a crucial resource for you and the adoptive parents during this period, not only to give support, but also to help solve problems and work together towards a solution.

Spending Time With Your Baby

"After I had the baby, I was still trying not to think about it because I was so tired and sore that crying aggravated everything. I felt like I was being torn apart. My heart felt like a thousand tiny glass shards."

"I felt so very heartbroken, even though I knew it was still for the best. The fact that he has the very best parents (and a wonderful birthmother and sisters) makes the pain subside and overcomes all the darkness and emptiness I feel."

"I didn't know it would hurt so much!"

Countless birthparents tell us they never imagined the joy and the pain they would feel after the birth of their child—joy from the extraordinary experience of seeing their baby for the first time, and pain from knowing they will soon be separated. Women who never wanted to parent find themselves falling in love with their baby. You may need more or less time in the hospital with your baby than you had originally planned. A change in plans after the birth doesn't necessarily mean a change of heart about your adoption plan. While some women fear that spending time with the baby in the hospital will make their separation unbearable, spending time with your baby may help you reconfirm your adoption decision.

"I was able to spend two days with my son after he was born. They were two of the most important days of my life. He was so tiny and precious. I spent time just looking at him . . ."

You may hear a lot about bonding during this time. The adoptive parents might be fearful that if you "bond" with your baby, you might not be able to place him for adoption. However, you already have bonded with your baby during your pregnancy, and being with your baby will help you either reconfirm or reconsider your decision. Some women are clear that they do not want to spend time with their baby at all and that decision is legitimate also. Your hospital stay may be very brief: twenty-four to forty-eight hours for an uncomplicated vaginal delivery and three to five days for a cesarean section. If you think you need more time with your baby before discharge, there are some alternatives you may want to consider:

- Some hospitals may allow a bit more time if it can be medically justified. Talk to your doctor to see if this can be arranged.
- You may want to spend the night in a hotel with the birthfather, a close friend, or a family member and your baby.
- You may decide to take your baby home for a day or two before placing him with the adoptive parents.
- You may be able to place your baby in a voluntary care home for a brief period of time, where you can visit and have more time to make your decision.

For the most part, birthmothers feel comfortable sending their baby home with the parents they have chosen. They did the preparation necessary to follow through with separating from the baby in the hospital. The decision not to connect physically with the baby after birth may facilitate the separation for some women. However, if you do feel strongly conflicted, take whatever time you need before taking the momentous step of placing your baby with the adoptive parents. Although some birthmothers do limit the amount of time they spend with their baby in the hospital and report feeling content and satisfied, one of the most common comments we hear from birthmoms is that they wish they had spent more time with their babies.

Naming Your Baby

After your delivery and before you leave the hospital, you will be asked to fill out your baby's birth certificate. The original birth certificate will have your name and the name you choose for your baby. Some states also include the birthfather's name. You may put any name you wish on the original birth certificate, including one of your own choosing or the one the adoptive parents selected. When the adoption is finalized, the name the adoptive parents choose will be on the revised birth certificate. If you want a copy of the original birth certificate, be sure to request it before the adoption is finalized since, in most states, all the adoption records will then be sealed.

Transitioning Your Baby to the Adoptive Parents

Your hospital stay is not only a time to spend with your baby, it is also a time to transition him to the adoptive parents. Seeing the adoptive parents with your baby gives you a chance to check out how it feels to see them together. Some birthparents choose to be the primary caretakers of their baby during the hospital stay, while others choose to share caretaking or let the adoptive parents care for the baby in the nursery. Allowing the adoptive parents time alone with the baby is a way you can show your trust and confidence in them, and it will allow them some time to start connecting with the new baby they will soon be parenting.

This is an emotionally charged time for the adoptive parents also. It is often the culmination of years of highs and lows, infertility treatments, and possibly other unsuccessful attempts to adopt. Adoptive parents are sometimes uncertain about how they should express their feelings and fear if they are overly expressive and involved with the baby, they may offend you. On the other hand, if they back off too much emotionally, you may think they aren't excited or committed to the adoption. Remember that they are also experiencing an enormously significant event and may not know exactly how to express their feelings. Being able to communicate with each other during this highly emotional time is of the utmost importance. By communicating to the adoptive parents your devotion to them and your confidence in their parenting, you will go a long way in strengthening your relationship.

Dealing with Others during Your Hospital Stay

"My hospital stay was very relaxed. I felt like everyone was supportive, including the adoptive parents, and they understood that I didn't need any extra stress. The hospital staff was respectful and supportive."

"I can describe my time in the hospital in two words:

ABSOLUTELY HORRIFYING. The nurses were sarcastic, and the doctor was a complete creep. If I had known what it was going to be like, I would have done the whole thing at home with a midwife."

During your hospital stay, your friends and family members may be involved and want to visit, participate, or give advice. Think about choosing an advocate during this time—someone whose only investment is making sure your needs are being met and who can communicate your wishes to others. Conflicts can occur with any of the following people:

The Adoptive Parents: They may make a comment that sounds hurtful, even though it is not their intent. Calling your baby "my" baby in front of you, not checking in with you before holding, feeding, or changing the baby, or asking their family to visit without your permission are some examples of things the adoptive parents may do that irritate or even anger you. Communication is key during this time. If you think the adoptive parents are being insensitive, talk to them, or ask a friend, social worker, or nurse to talk to them. Most adoptive parents are just nervous or excited and will respond to someone gently pointing out ways to change their behavior.

The Birthfather: For many birthfathers, seeing the baby for the first time is when reality really hits. The physical resemblance and the unique feelings that babies evoke may cause a birthfather to reconsider his decision. There have been occasions where the birthfather did not participate in the adoption planning, yet he came to the hospital after the birth. This may also be the first time the birthfather meets the adoptive parents, which can be awkward for all involved.

Your Relatives and Friends: Even though they are well meaning, your family and friends may make comments that cause you distress: "Your baby is soooo cute! I don't know how you can give him away." or "Are you sure you should be spending so much time with her? It's just going to make it harder to give her up." You may be inclined to try and please others, even when it's not what you want. You may also feel you need to entertain and take care of your visitors, when you really just want to hold your baby or take a nap. It might be wise to talk beforehand with friends and relatives who will be coming to visit you to educate them a little about open adoption and let them know about your hospital plans. This is a time when you need a lot of support and encouragement, and it is definitely not a time for taking care of the needs of others. Your family and friends may be overwhelmed by their own feelings. Your parents may be especially affected by seeing you (their baby!) in a situation that is emotionally painful. They will feel some deep grief for the grandchild they are losing.

Doctors, Nurses, Social Workers, Roommates: Hopefully, most of the people caring for you during your hospital stay will be very sensitive. If you toured the hospital prior to your delivery, you will have had the opportunity to meet some of the hospital staff. Most hospitals appreciate knowing about your plans beforehand so the staff can be alerted to your needs. We have heard, however, about well-meaning hospital staff or hospital roommates who made insensitive comments or questioned some birthmothers' choices. To prevent rooming with another mother and baby, if you suspect this will make you feel uncomfortable, you could talk to your doctor or the medical social worker in advance to try and arrange a private room.

Leaving the Hospital

"I videotaped a good-bye to Jeff after he was born. I held him and said why I was doing this and told him I loved him. It was very healing."

Your time in the hospital will come to an end more quickly than you anticipated. If you are placing your baby with the adoptive parents when you leave the hospital, it will be a momentous time. You will be saying farewell to your baby, not forever necessarily, but as your baby's mother. Other birthmoms may be saying good-bye without any plans to stay in touch or connect. You've been with her for the last nine months, and even though it felt at times like this day would never come, when it finally does, you may wish it never had. You are not only facing the prospect of leaving with empty arms, you are in the midst of a role change: no longer mom, but birthmom. As much as you have prepared for this day, you may feel totally unprepared for the enormity of the feelings. You may be in a lot of physical discomfort, as well as being emotionally drained, and this isn't the time to be shy about asking for help. Some birthparents ask the adoptive parents to take them home, and spend time with them and the baby after leaving the hospital. Give some thought to these possibilities, even if you aren't sure what you will need, physically or emotionally.

Depending on the state and type of adoption you are going through (agency or independent), you will most likely have to sign some paperwork before leaving the hospital. Some agencies require you to sign a relinquishment or put the baby into foster care. Make sure you thoroughly check out any papers that you are asked to sign. You can have an attorney review any document before signing. Hopefully, you will have been introduced to any expected paperwork prior to the day of discharge from the hospital. At the very least, you can anticipate signing a form that allows the adoptive parents to care for the baby medically until she is legally theirs.

Ceremonies

Some birth and adoptive parents prepare and participate in rituals or ceremonies to honor the new family they are creating. This can be done while still at the hospital, or shortly after leaving. A ceremony can be spiritual or not, and it can occur in a church, a hospital chapel, a park, your home, the adoptive family's home, or any place that has significance for you. Some examples of ceremonies are:

- Everyone lights a candle and makes a wish for the baby and for each other. The birthparents light the candle first, then pass it on to the adoptive parents.
- A minister, spiritual advisor, or friend says a prayer or makes a special offering for the baby, the adoptive parents, the birthparents, and their families.
- A special poem is read or a song is sung.
- Some churches have dedications for adopted babies, with the birthparents and adoptive parents participating.

Relinquishing Your Rights

Your legal rights to your child will remain intact until you sign a relinquishment or consent to adoption. Agencies require a relinquishment, while independent adoptions require a consent to adoption. Regardless of the type of adoption, you cannot relinquish your rights as a birthmother until after the birth. (Some states allow the birthfather to sign forms allowing the adoption to proceed prior to the birth, but the birthmother can only sign a consent or relinquishment after the birth.) Some agencies and attorneys may ask you to sign an "intent to place," meaning that you are planning to place your baby for adoption. This is not a legal consent, however, and is usually only used in the very rare instances that a birthmother disappears after placement and cannot be located to sign a final relinquishment.

We think it is enormously helpful to review all the consent/relinquishment paperwork prior to the birth of your baby. The language in the forms can sound quite harsh, especially if you are reading it for the first time soon after the birth of your baby. Reviewing the paperwork with your attorney or counselor will familiarize you with the language at a time when you may be less emotional and will allow you more time to ask questions. Although many agencies are required to give you the relinquishment paperwork prior to the final signing, make sure your counselor sits down and thoroughly reviews the forms with you. Many young women have told us that while they were emotionally prepared to sign the relinquishment or consent, they were caught off guard by the length and language in the paperwork.

If you are placing your child through an independent adoption, your attorney or adoption counselor can obtain copies of the consent paperwork to review prior to the final signing.

A Change of Heart

After the birth of your baby, your emotions and love for the baby may overwhelm you, and you may find yourself reconsidering your decision to place your baby with the adoptive parents. Most birthparents go through a time when they reconsider their decision, especially after the birth. This is very normal. If you are having doubts about your decision, talk to someone you trust. You might be getting pressure from everyone around you, but it's crucial to think about you and your baby. Some of the questions and issues to consider if you are having a change of heart are:

• Since I made my original adoption plan, has anything changed in my life that makes parenting a better option?

- Will there be a change in the support being offered to me if I choose to parent this baby?
- Is the birthfather now encouraging me to parent, and is this a good decision for my baby and me?
- Am I willing to make a decision now, in a very short time, that will undo a decision I've been working on for many months?

If your change of plans is based solely on the intense feelings that have surfaced since your baby's birth, you might want to take time to sit with your feelings for a while. If you are reconsidering your decision, though, you need to let the adoptive parents know, and if you can't talk to them alone, you might want to ask your counselor, the social worker at the hospital, or a trusted friend to help you. Most adoptive parents are incredibly anxious during this time, and if you are really changing your mind, it is only fair to let them know as soon as possible. You might want to consider temporary foster care, taking your baby home for a few days, or having a friend or relative care for your baby until you are surer about your decision. As hard as this may seem for everyone, it is much more difficult to place a baby with the adoptive parents and then change your mind and take your baby back.

> *"My decision to place my baby for adoption was made on sound reasoning. Though after her birth I would have loved to parent her, I knew nothing in my life or circumstances had changed, and I still could not give her the things I desired for her, except by placing her into her parents' home. What I did not anticipate was the love I would feel for her parents and the great longing I had to put my arms around them and say thank you. Even today, I trust that they have done and will continue to do a great job. I may never have the chance to meet her or her parents again, but I still have that trust in my heart."*

Chapter 7:
GRIEF, LOSS AND HEALING

The loss of a child, no matter how that loss has come about, brings very profound pain and sadness. The first few days or even weeks after you place your child with his new parents might be the most emotional you have ever experienced. Sometimes the sadness does not come right away. Some women consciously try not to feel their loss until they have achieved some distance from it—maybe at a later date, when they can no longer change their minds. Other women, busy in their lives, keep telling themselves they don't have time to think about it. Still others are afraid to let themselves feel the sadness for fear they will feel it too deeply and won't be able to recover. Of course, many birthmothers simply succumb to their feelings and spend a lot of time letting themselves cry until there are no more tears.

Adoption is a phenomenon created by society that involves loss for each member of the adoption triad. For adoptive parents, the loss lies in the absence of the idealized birthchild, the loss of their bloodlines, the loss of a jointly conceived child, and the loss of privacy and control. The adoptee loses the chance to grow up in his original family, and often his original culture. For the birthparent, the loss is easy to see—losing a child that you conceived, carried within your body, and brought into this world. While adoption, then, is a new baby for the adoptive parents, a new family for the adoptee, and the solution to a problem for the birth parent, it is also loss, loss, loss.

Grief is an emotion that we, as a culture, are not very comfortable with. We dislike feeling sad and we have a hard time knowing how to help those who are mourning. Yet grief is one of the most commonly experienced emotions. Everyone experiences loss. Loss comes in many forms, from small everyday losses like losing your keys to the major ones like losing a job, breaking up with your partner, divorce or death. And each loss carries with it a grieving process. While we have rituals around death, most other losses are not formally recognized, which only reinforces the feeling of unreality that surrounds the grieving process of adoption.

Birthparent loss and grief has traditionally been ignored and only recently has the importance of grieving the loss been talked about and encouraged. Historically, birthparents have been told to "get on with your life." Since placing a child for adoption was regarded in society as a positive outcome to an unfortunate situation, there was often an assumption that the results for the birthparent were positive as well and there was very little, if any, post-placement counseling for birthparents.

Fortunately, this situation has changed significantly, as birthparents have become more vocal about their needs and about the long-term effects of unresolved grieving. Most adoption agencies are now very sensitive to the issues of post-adoption loss and counselors are trained in grief counseling. There are also many therapists who have worked with birthparents and are attuned to the issue of post-placement bereavement.

Everyone grieves in her own way. There really is no right or wrong way, no one prescription that will make the hurt go away. Grief has a way of taking its own path. Grieving is really part of the recovery process. In fact, grief is such a universally experienced emotion that it has been much studied. One particular theory of grief identifies five common themes or "stages."

The Five Stages of Grief and Loss

- Denial
- Anger
- Bargaining
- Sadness/Depression
- Acceptance/Resolution

Elizabeth Kubler-Ross, in her groundbreaking book, **On Death and Dying**, talks about the fluidity of these stages:

Denial: Simply stated, this is the part where you consciously or unconsciously refuse to accept the reality of what is happening because it is too painful and you are not ready to face the hurt. The numbness you may feel after the birth is a normal response to the loss you are experiencing. This can be experienced physically as a lack of feeling or detachment — almost as if you were in another body or another world. You may think, "This is a dream — I'm really going to wake up soon." Denial, if it keeps you from necessary action, can be detrimental. However, denial also helps you because it can temporarily protect you from emotions that are too strong for you to handle at the moment.

Anger: Once denial has been overcome, anger is often the next emotion. Anger is therefore a movement toward health because you are starting to take in the reality of the situation. Anger can be focused inward, and sometimes this results in hurting oneself through dangerous acts and risk-taking behavior. Anger can also be directed toward family, friends, the adoptive parents, your counselor or lawyer, or the birthfather. Anger can find its expression in many ways, both healthy and unhealthy. Anger or rage is a natural reaction to resisting reality, but it is also an emotion filled with power and energy. There is seductiveness about the feeling of anger because unlike the numbness of denial and the ache of sadness, it is a feeling full of intensity and force.

Bargaining: This goes something like, "Please God, if you would just let me not be pregnant—just this one time—I will never, ever, ever have sex again until I am married! Please?" While bargaining is a recognition of reality, it also involves a sort of grasping-at-straws desperation, based on the hope that maybe it could be different with divine intervention. It is an attempt to change or alter the outcome of events and can involve some obsessive thinking about the past. Bargaining is a way, albeit temporary, to delay the inevitable sadness which usually follows.

Sadness and Depression: Once the fireworks of anger have subsided, the embers of sadness remain. Sadness is an acknowledgment of the permanent change that has been brought into your life—the beginning of an understanding that you can't have things the way they used to be ever again. Depression and sadness can take many forms, physically and emotionally. Interspersed with the sadness may be intense feelings of guilt — that you didn't consider all you options more carefully, that you chose adoption because you had certain goals you wanted to pursue at this time of your life (i.e. school, career). Sadness is usually the most difficult part of the grieving process because it is so hard to remain in pain. It may be the time when you feel the most alone and the time when you most question your decision. Recognizing your grief and accepting your pain without judgement can be your first step toward acceptance.

Acceptance and Resolution: Denial, bargaining, anger, and sadness are all a part of achieving acceptance. Acceptance is the acknowledgment that you have done all you can, and that now you must find a way to live your life in order to survive, and yes, to flourish. Acceptance also acknowledges that there are some things in this world over which we have no control—namely the past. Acceptance does not mean that you will never feel sad about your decision. You will feel some poignancy throughout your life about having placed your child for adoption. But you will also experience a new sense of peace and hope as you adjust to your loss.

Physical, Emotional and Behavioral Reactions to Loss

When people talk about grieving, they are often referring to the sad feelings that accompany a loss. Grief reactions, however, can include physical and behavioral symptoms in addition to the emotional ones. Remember that grief is a **normal** response to an "abnormal" situation, and your body will also respond. Some of the more common symptoms of grieving include:

- Confusion, disorientation, forgetfulness, spacing out
- Difficulties with concentration and focus
- Excessive worry
- Sleep disorders, recurring dreams or nightmares

- Extreme exhaustion, even if you are getting enough sleep
- Changes in appetite
- Increase in smoking, alcohol or drug use
- Difficulty making decisions
- Clouded judgement
- Numbness and inability to express your feelings
- Mood swings (from euphoria to depression)
- Irritability, resentment, frustration, anger
- Anxiety and panic
- Apathy, isolation, loneliness, vulnerability
- Headaches, dizziness, muscle aches, stomach aches
- Conflicts with people in your life
- Keeping excessively busy to avoid feelings

While any of these reactions can be in response to mourning, physical symptoms should always be checked out with your doctor.

101 Doubts, Behaviors, and Paranoid Thoughts That Prove You Are a Normal Birthmother

The period of time after you place your child for adoption is filled with emotions: doubt, guilt, happiness, fear, hope, sadness, shame, listlessness, self-retribution, relief, and confusion. There are so many questions: What can I expect to feel afterwards? How long will I hurt? What do other birthmothers feel? Is it normal to feel so angry? What does it say about me if I feel happy and relieved? Will I ever stop thinking about my child? Am I having a nervous break-down?

These are questions asked by most birthparents. In order to help you make some sense of how you might feel, we have put together a timeline describing some characteristic grief reactions during the first year. Grieving is not a linear process — it is much more jagged. You will go back and forth through the stages and may find yourself feeling like it's the first week when it's really been six months. The intensity of your feelings will ebb and flow as life progresses and you will experience and re-experience many of the feelings described below. We hope you will be able to find yourself somewhere on this list—but don't worry if your feelings are not exactly under the right month! The most important thing about your recovery is that you are moving forward.

The recovery timeline is intended to describe a spiraling process, not a straight line. **Please note this is meant only as a guide.**

GRIEF RESPONSES DURING
THE FIRST YEAR

The First Week:
- You are overwhelmed with love for your baby.
- Crying every day is typical.
- You ache for the baby to be with you.
- You have obsessive thoughts about the baby missing you.
- Constant worrying that the baby is not okay.
- You are numb, tired and hurt all over.
- Postpartum depression.

The First Six Weeks:
- Crying in spurts—anything will set you off.
- You feel like a part of you is missing.
- You notice lots of babies and children; all the movies on TV are about children and adoption.
- You feel different from a lot of the people you used to feel comfortable around; they seem immature, superficial.
- If you have a tendency toward alcohol or drug abuse, you may feel a craving for overdoing it.
- You may reevaluate your decision to place your baby.
- You may begin to second-guess your choice in adoptive parents. Why do you think you know them or can trust them?
- Feelings of great sadness, heaviness, fatigue, anxiety, irritability and sleep disturbances are common.
- You try to move forward, but all the plans you once looked forward to don't sound as good anymore—you forget why you chose adoption.
- You also feel relief and elation at your accomplishment—you feel proud of yourself.
- You hold on to thoughts of your baby.

By Three Months:

- You still feel sadness and think of the baby often, but the intensity of the sadness is lessening.
- Your body is starting to recover and you have more energy.
- If you have contact with the adoptive family and baby, the pictures or visits can create conflicting emotions.
- You are beginning to feel some optimism about the future and hold out some hope that you will be OK.
- Just as you feel a little more stable, you approach the time when you got pregnant last year—this brings back many memories and could trigger feelings of hopelessness.
- As you start to heal, you may experience feelings of guilt.

By Six Months:

- A period of time goes by (this could be a minute, an hour or a day) and you notice you haven't thought about the baby—you wonder if you are forgetting about her.
- If you are still experiencing intense sadness, you might wonder if there's something wrong with you, especially if you are around people who are uncomfortable with your pain.
- You are feeling some periods of acceptance interspersed with the sadness.
- Your sadness is no longer a stranger to you and the pain feels a little softer.
- You might even find yourself laughing or wanting to go out with your friends, something you couldn't even imagine doing a few months ago.

At One Year:

- The baby's first birthday—you remember all you've been through.
- You may feel anger, sadness, regret and/or depression with a severity you hadn't expected.
- You are aware that you will never be the same.
- You are starting to get your life back and think about the future—your future.

Moving through Your Grief toward Acceptance and Healing

The grieving process does not magically come to a halt at the end of the first year. Grief counselors say that grieving continues well beyond the first year and that a prolonged grief response to a difficult loss is not abnormal. The first year is significant, though, because for many, it is most intense. When the first year comes to a close, you will have experienced all the important anniversary dates once (i.e. finding out you were pregnant, making your adoption decision, giving birth, placing your baby with the adoptive parents and going through the holidays). You will have achieved some distance and hopefully some moments of peace and acceptance.

In the stages of grieving, you probably recognized some of the emotions you experienced during your pregnancy and birth. You may still be going through some of those stages. The grieving process is fluid and you will drift in and out of different feelings over time. You may experience anger, sadness, or even denial again and again throughout your life. No one moves neatly through these emotions; there is no definite beginning or end. You can expect adoption-related feelings to resurface as you travel through certain passages in your journey of life.

Grieving is hard work. It takes time and patience. It involves paying to attention to your emotions, being compassionate toward yourself and accepting your feelings without judgement. By allowing your feeling to exist, you can begin the process of healing. Your healing will reflect your individuality, your previous losses and how you mourned them, your upbringing and culture, your life situation, your supports and your strength. Just as people recover from physical injury at different rates and in different ways, individuals heal from emotional injury in their own distinctive ways. Because you are healing faster than other birthmothers you know doesn't necessarily mean that you are in denial. And healing more slowly doesn't necessary mean that you don't want to move forward. Your friends, family and acquaintances may have suggestions or even unsolicited advice about your healing processes. However, in the end, you are the one who must be comfortable with the pace of your own recovery. Being able to accept the particular feelings at the time they occur is one of the most important tools in the healing process. If you are feeling sad or angry, guilty or numb, and can acknowledge these emotions, as distressing as they may be, you will find that you are progressing. It is hard to stay in sadness for any period of time, but acceptance and compassion toward yourself is central to your recovery.

Unresolved and Complicated Grieving

Unresolved grief refers to grief that is repressed or denied for a very long time. There is very little acknowledgement of the loss and no movement toward acceptance and healing. This may occur because the loss is extremely intense or painful and the person has no support or ability to express a range of emotions. Or perhaps the person feels afraid and unequipped to handle the enormity of the feelings and suppresses all their painful emotions. Some people fear that if they start crying, they will never stop or that anger is just not an appropriate emotion to express.

We are not taught how to deal with our grief, and the unfortunate consequence is that the sad feelings are often ignored or pushed under. People hold onto their grief for a variety of reasons, and often are not even aware that they are still grieving for a loss that occurred years before. Several losses close together or important losses that were not mourned significantly can complicate the grief. Unresolved grief can compromise your life. The grieving that is suppressed may take the form of anger or blame, physical ailments, addictions, job difficulties or relationship problems. If you feel that you have been unable to express your emotions or that you are stuck in a particular stage of grieving and are concerned that you are not moving forward, see a therapist who specializes in grief work.

How Do I Know If I Need Help?

There are times when birthmothers find that their lives are not moving forward, and that, in fact, they are more depressed than ever. You really are the best judge of how you are doing. What may be normal for someone else may not be normal for you. It is always appropriate to ask a professional—a counselor, psychologist, psychiatrist, or medical doctor—for help evaluating your emotional health. Most likely, you will be given the reassurance that what you are experiencing is normal and okay, but there are cases where medical or psychiatric intervention may be needed in order to help you over the "humps" of recovery.

Will I Be All Right Someday?

If you are like the vast majority of birthmothers we have worked with, you will be able to ride out the turbulence of your emotions and move forward with your life. Life is all about change and loss, making decisions and living with the consequences, and being able to move toward a life of peace and fulfillment. You will do all of these things in your own time. Meanwhile, here are some ways to be kind to you:

Give yourself time. Allow yourself time to recover. This is true for any healing process. If you push yourself too soon or set up unrealistic expectations, you will only feel worse when you cannot meet them.

Allow for changes in your life. Many birthmoms expect to return to their old lives immediately. All the things they looked forward to doing after the baby—dating, parties, school, a new job, moving—often don't have the same meaning they once did. In fact, most birthmoms feel they have matured faster than many of their friends and no longer feel they belong to the same crowd. You have changed. Allow yourself time to figure out how the "new you" wants to live life.

Seek support from friends who will listen without judgement. Take care of yourself by being with friends who will let you talk about how you feel without trying to fix you. It is all right to avoid friends who cannot understand at this time. You might even want to give someone you trust—a close friend, your boyfriend, husband, mother, sister, or roommate—the job of running interference for you. They can take phone messages, answer the door for you, and protect you in general from the people you are not ready to see.

Don't overdo it. Take on one new thing at a time. Some birthmoms feel they have to radically change their life right after placing a child for adoption. This is generally not the time to uproot yourself or plunge into wildly unfamiliar territory. It is good to do things that make you feel productive or move you toward accomplishing goals, such as starting back to school or finding a job, but avoid making major decisions or taking on too much at once.

Remember your hormones! You just had a baby. As if that weren't difficult enough, you are now left with a body that is changing rapidly. Your breasts are probably sore and leaky, you may have stitches, your abdomen is stretched and saggy, you may have a few more pounds on you than you would like, and on top of all this, your hormones are going crazy. It is no wonder you are feeling out of control.

Call the adoptive parents. Depending on your relationship with the adoptive parents and the agreement you worked out with them for contact after the placement, it can be reassuring to hear their voices and find out how the baby is doing.

Talk to another birthmother. Someone else who has been through placing a child for adoption can be extremely comforting during times when you are feeling down.

Seek counseling. Arrange regular counseling contacts after your placement. Sometimes it helps to talk to someone you don't have to explain yourself to, someone you don't have to "be strong for." If you don't already have a counselor, please consider getting one. It is not too late.

Make yourself do one uplifting thing a week. It may be as silly as painting your toenails fire engine red, renting a movie, taking a walk, or smiling at yourself in the mirror. You'll work up to bigger things.

Nurture your spirit. You could attend a place of worship, meditate or take a yoga class. You could listen to a soothing tape, read something inspirational or just sit in the sun in a place you love and reflect on the beauty of the world.

When to Ask for Professional Help

- Anytime you feel stuck or unable to more forward in your grieving.
- If you feel you have no one to turn to for support.
- If, after one month, you are still only wearing pajamas.
- If, after three months, you still believe you have no future.
- If, after six months, you cry most of the time.
- Any time you have thoughts of suicide.

Beware of Drugs and Alcohol

If you had a problem in the past with alcohol or drug abuse, the period right after placing your child for adoption is a very fragile time. It is not uncommon for birthmothers to turn to alcohol or drugs to try and dull the pain or elevate themselves out of their sadness. We must caution you about coping in this fashion. While drinking or using drugs may temporarily ease your sadness, they only hinder your natural grieving process. Treating your pain through substance abuse only delays the inevitable and usually makes it worse by creating another problem.

Good Grief!

After all is said and done, grief is good! Grieving is a way to measure change, and change is a way to measure growth. Growth is an essential element of living a vibrant, mature, and meaningful life. Give yourself an honor badge for being a survivor.

Chapter 8:
THE FIRST YEAR

The first year after placing a child for adoption can seem like a lifetime in itself. You will pass through various stages, look at things from different angles, and experience a multitude of feelings, all within that first year (Many birthparents report that they get through their most difficult times emotionally within the first few months after relinquishment, although some take much longer.). One's experience of and response to the grieving process is very personal, and there is no "right" time frame to adhere to. Grief is one of those feelings that just has to unfold naturally, according to your own personal needs. Any attempt to force or deny or hurry or criticize the grieving will only obstruct the natural healing. The first year after placement is a time to be kind and patient with yourself. Rather than judging yourself as you adjust to your life "post-adoption," it may be more useful to act as your own "gentle witness"; just observe the various feelings or moods without evaluation.

Intertwined with the grieving process, other issues will unfold during your first year after placement. Your relationship with the adoptive parents will continue along its own course. Immediately after the birth, your relationship may undergo a strong "stress test" on trust. This is especially true when the adoptive parents take the child home from the hospital before you actually sign the relinquishment papers, terminating your parental rights. Each state has different requirements regarding when you must sign, and it is essential that you are familiar with all your state's laws surrounding relinquishment. However, in most cases, the adoptive parents take the baby home from the hospital and begin parenting before the baby is legally theirs.

The Shift in Relationship

"I had my baby on December twenty-first, and boy, that was some depressing Christmas! When I could stop feeling sorry for all that I was missing, I thought about what a wonderful Christmas present I had given my baby—a new family that could provide everything she needed."

No matter how confident and secure you are with the adoption, you will again reevaluate your decision before you relinquish. It is important to remember that most adoptive couples have come to this place having undergone some disappointments. No reassurance in the world on your part will completely convince them they have nothing to worry about in terms of you changing your mind. They need to be realistic—you cannot completely predict how you will feel about your adoption decision until the child is actually born and the time for saying good-bye arrives. But they also have to feel free to begin loving the baby without reservation and feel like his parents from the moment they take him home. This anxiety is not your responsibility, but your response to their fears can go a long way toward paving a trusting relationship. They also need a trusting relationship with a counselor, someone they can share their insecurities with so as not to burden you at a time when you have your own strong feelings.

Similarly, this is a time when the adoptive parents are in a position to positively affect the trusting nature of your future relationship. No matter how strongly they communicate their commitment to you and to the openness of your relationship, you may still fear they will lose interest in you once they begin parenting the baby. One of the most difficult realities to adjust to after the birth is the fact that the child will replace you in many ways as the main focus for the adoptive family. This is natural and to be expected, but it can still be painful. It is important for the parents to be sensitive to you and your needs at this time and work with you to help smooth your transition from being the mother to being the birthmother. You might notice yourself having strong negative reactions to the adoptive parents at this time, like feelings of rejection or anger. Talking about your mutual expectations for the first few months in advance is highly recommended.

It has been our experience that contact immediately after the placement can be very reassuring for all concerned. Oftentimes, birthparents will not feel comfortable calling adoptive parents for fear they might be perceived as "intruding," but they'll be very curious about how the baby is doing and how the family is adjusting to its newest member. The adoptive parents will also hesitate to call the birthparents, despite their concern and affection for them, for fear their phone call will "pour salt in the wound" of an already painful situation. In some adoptions, both birth and adoptive parents agree that a "transition period" without contact is the best arrangement for all involved. This may help the adoptive parents focus on the child and their new role as parents, and it may also help the birthparents begin to separate from the baby. Whatever your personal decision, it helps to discuss and clarify each person's expectations before disappointments or misunderstandings occur.

Rage and Resentment

A fairly typical, yet disturbing reaction is often described as rage, resentment, or jealousy toward the adoptive parents. Seeing the baby you carried and loved for nine months in the arms of your adoptive couple can evoke very strong feelings, especially in the beginning. The resentment may not make sense to you, but it is part of the loss experience. You might ask yourself, "Why do they get to keep my baby? How come they are so prepared financially or emotionally that they are ready to parent? Why not me?" This is a time in the grief process when birthparents must continue to remember why they chose adoption in the first place—usually for the well being of the baby. You may ask yourself, "If this is such a good decision, why does it feel so bad?" Birthmothers need to remind themselves of making a conscious choice: Long-term gain for short-term pain, as opposed to short-term gain for long-term pain. In other words, they chose tremendous sadness in the present with the belief that, ultimately, adoption would prove the best choice for their child and for themselves.

"Boy, was I a basket case! Before the birth, I just wanted to get it over with and move on with my life. I tried not to think about the baby so I would not get attached. After the birth, I was torn apart. I couldn't stand seeing them with my son, and I hated them. Everything they said irritated me. I just wanted to hold my son and never let him go. I was so confused."

Trust and Transition

This post-placement period is terribly important in a number of ways. As mentioned before, the trust you feel for one another will be put to the test under circumstances where the emotional investment is at its highest. The adoptive family has a natural need for "permission" to begin bonding as a family. You may need some reassurance that they will honor their future agreements with you. Your relationship with the adoptive parents will shift as you establish new roles with one another; the friendship and closeness you have been feeling may change shape. Your relationship with the birthfather may go through changes, too, if you have been working together to complete the adoption. These adjustments are not necessarily unwelcome, but they are hard to predict and hard to imagine. Like any ongoing relationship, there will be growing pains as you, the birthfather, the adoptive couple, and eventually the child evolve in your relation to one another. This is true whether or not there is actual physical contact after the placement. Even if you choose no ongoing contact, there will still be a relationship between you, the parents you have selected, and the child.

Pain and Growth

Painful experiences can also be the gateway to growth. In the midst of your great sorrow, you may not believe this. It can be terribly annoying when well-meaning friends or family members tell you that the adoption can provide you the opportunity to make changes in your life. Or that you should be proud of yourself for doing such an unselfish thing. However, there is some inherent truth to the notion that the most difficult experiences can offer us the occasion for a very deep level of insight and reflection. Perhaps sadness allows us to retreat from the intense, hectic pace of our life for a moment and we notice things that we didn't see before. Or maybe the intensity of loss makes us much more aware of those things in life that we cherish and helps up redefine what is truly important. You may notice that you have much less interest in trivial matters and that there is a depth to your life that you weren't aware of before your adoption. This doesn't mean that life has to take on a morose or deeply serious quality. On the contrary, you may find that you have a greater appreciation and love for those things that truly matter to you.

Your New Path

> *"My counselor now tells me that I used to say the grieving was worse than I expected, although I don't remember saying that now. I think I felt better by the third month, but having the opportunity to see Chad and his parents a few times throughout the first year really helped. He looked so happy and well adjusted. Seeing them just reconfirmed that I absolutely made the right choice."*

> *"What helped me during the first year, believe it or not, was feeling free to be sad or cry whenever I wanted. Also, I tried to think of what was best for my little girl. Keeping her in the foreground of my mind was the biggest help."*

> *"The agony of losing my child has never gotten better. It has been hard for me to continue on with my life, and it's already been nine months! Sometimes I wonder if I really made the right decision."*

The first year following the adoption is really an opportunity for you to begin regaining some feeling of normalcy in your life. It is a time for you to experiment with different ways of relating to yourself, to others, and to the adoptive parents. It may mean returning to school and continuing with your educational goals, returning to work, continuing to parent other children, or beginning a new career or relationship. Many birthparents use the placement as a turning point in their lives or an inspiration to begin something new. During the first year, you will discover to whom you can talk about your experience. You may begin a new intimate relationship, and you will need to decide how much of your adoption story to share with the new people that enter your life. You will be faced with difficult questions like, "What happened to your baby?" and possibly insensitive comments from people who do not support your choice. Your family members will be experiencing their own grief concerning the baby, which can sometimes complicate how you feel.

A common feeling that younger birthmothers experience is that they have grown up so fast. They feel so much more mature than a lot of their friends and begin to feel distanced from them.

"Everything these girls at school talk about seems so stupid, so trivial. It's like they're looking at the world through rose-colored glasses. I keep feeling like there's no going back for me. I can never go back to the way it was before."

Hopefully, you will have begun to surround yourself with people who can confirm what you chose to do. The first year becomes a time to discover on whom you can really depend. Remember to bolster your support system around certain holidays like Christmas, Mother's Day, Father's Day, or the baby's first birthday. Anticipate the mood swings that may accompany these times of year.

Am I a Mom or Not?

After the birth and placement of your baby, you may need to try to redefine your identity. For months you have been an expectant mother, the pregnant woman, the mother-to-be. Once you are no longer pregnant or parenting, it may be hard to remember all the other wonderful things that make up who you are! Reconnecting with activities or people that interest you will help remind you of all the other parts of yourself. Some birthmothers struggle with the question, Am I a mom or not? This is a very personal question and one that different women will answer differently. Although you are not parenting your child, you are one of his two mothers. Whether you choose to refer to yourself as a mother or not is a choice only you can make, but you are certainly your child's birthmother. A very difficult part of placing a child for adoption is clarifying your role. You are no longer the parent of the child. Part of the grieving process involves relinquishing the role of being a parent. Even birthmothers who initially told us that they didn't want to be a mother are often surprised at how strongly they are affected by the loss of that identity. You can still offer wonderful things to your child as the birthparent, though. It will take some time to sort this out and develop a relationship based on your new role. If you have a trusting relationship with the adoptive parents, you can talk about how you see yourself in relation to them and to your birthchild.

Some women report that as time grows between the placement and the present, a sense of unreality begins to settle in. "Did this really happen to me? The adoption seems so far away, so unreal—like I watched it happening to someone else."

Contact during the First Year

Contact with the parents and baby during the first year can range from very closed to very open. The level of contact you agree on is a very personal choice that should remain flexible as people's feelings and expectations shift. You may agree you will not have any direct contact with one another. Or you may just want letters and pictures, perhaps an occasional phone call. Most adoptions today include some kind of ongoing physical contact, although the extent of the visits can be negotiated. Once a year? Two or four times a year? Every month? Arranged at everyone's convenience? When you are thinking about the kind of contact you envision, keep in mind it is the quality of the relationship that is important, not necessarily the quantity of visits. Feeling comfortable and clear about your roles with one another is paramount. Getting together should be a positive experience for all, and sometimes this takes some work and time. If the visits feel uncomfortable, you should consult with your counselor for some help in getting back on track or changing the structure. The spirit of openness, not just "open adoption," is the healthy goal.

Many birth and adoptive parents develop an agreement for post-placement contact prior to the birth and relinquishment of the baby. It is a good idea to review this agreement after six months or so, as everyone's wants and needs may change. It is very difficult to know what kind of contact feels right until after you have given birth and the adoptive parents have taken the baby home. Consider setting up a meeting with the adoptive parents so you can review your agreement. This is a way to negotiate changes and discuss conflict, misunderstanding or hurt feelings. It is also a time that you can reflect upon all the positive aspects of your adoption and your relationship with each other. Some questions and issues you could discuss at this get-together include:

- How has the contact felt (i.e. visits, pictures, telephone calls)? Do we want more or less contact?
- Are we comfortable discussing any conflict or issues directly, or do we need help from a counselor?
- What has been positive about our adoption? What things would we change if we could?
- How are our family members adjusting?
- Is there anything we could do for one another to enhance our relationship?
- How is the baby doing? And how are you doing as a family?

If the Adoptive Parents Won't Honor your Agreement for Contact

If you made a specific agreement for contact with the adoptive parents and they are not honoring their commitment, you should contact your adoption professional immediately. There are many reasons why adoptive parents might pull back. They might be fearful about you changing your mind, if the adoption is not finalized yet. They may be feeling insecure about your role as they are trying to develop their own roles as parents. They may be getting negative feedback from others about your ongoing relationship. They may need a break from their intense relationship with you so that they can settle down and get used to the changes their life is undergoing.

Many adoption agencies these days do extensive counseling with the adoptive parents to help them with the intensity of the post-placement period and most adoptive parents are committed to the relationship with you. A counseling session or two will offer you both the chance to discuss your fears and redefine your agreement. Historically, open adoption agreements have not been legally binding. However, the trend has been set by some state legislatures to file these agreements with adoption papers to legitimize the legality of such agreements. In other states, these agreements are based solely on your trust for one another.

If You Choose Not to Have Contact

Some people are very clear that open adoption is not for them. For a variety of reasons, they do not want ongoing contact. Some birthparents feel that not staying in touch will make it easier to get on with their lives and put the whole experience behind them. If you choose a closed adoption, make sure the agency, attorney, and adoptive parents understand what your expectations are and feel comfortable honoring them. Do some reading about the differences between open and closed adoptions, and give some thought to the possibility that your child might someday search for you. You have the right to choose the kind of adoption that best suits you, and that includes an adoption that is closed or semi-open.

Is Peace of Mind Possible?

Some birthparents report they feel stuck in their pain about the adoption, and time does not seem to be making a difference. One birthmom recalls,

> *"I kept thinking that my sadness was the only thing I had left connecting me to my daughter—I thought if I began to feel better, I would just lose her again."*

Some birthparents equate healing and feeling positive with feeling like they've abandoned their child. They think that somehow staying trapped in guilt or sadness is what they should do if they really love their child. Feeling at peace with your adoption plan and beginning to get on with your life is not the same thing as forgetting about your baby. You do not deserve to be unhappy, nor would your child want you to feel guilt or pain about your adoption plan. By the end of your first year, we hope you are feeling some acceptance and peace about the adoption. This does not mean you will not feel sad. But we hope that oneday you can honestly say you do not regret your decision or begrudge yourself for making it.

A little more than a year after placing her son for adoption, a young woman describes how she has fared emotionally:

> *"At very first I was really happy and gung-ho on being there and having it really open. After a few months I started to wonder about what it would be like if I had kept him and I got a little depressed. Now I am really content with the decision I made. I know it was the best decision for everyone involved. I hope to become closer to them than I am right now. I want to be really involved in my son's life. I want him to know exactly why I chose what I did and that I still love him no matter what."*

Chapter 9:
BEYOND THE FIRST YEAR

"I am very happy I went through with the adoption. I can see what a great child she is and how great they are as a family."

"There are days that are still hard for me, and I still feel such sadness."

"The grieving process . . . I just wasn't prepared for the duration. My son is now three years old, and I am still experiencing the loss and grief. I've never once regretted my decision, but I do miss seeing him. He lives in New York now, though, so it's a little harder to visit."

When the first year following relinquishment comes to an end, you might expect that your feelings of grief would begin to fade. While it is true that the first year is often filled with sharp, intense pain, regret and longing, the feelings in the subsequent years have been described by some as a dull ache, punctuated by periodic stabs of pain. For some birthmothers, the fact that they have given birth to a child, and then forever disconnected from that child, is an awareness that is never far from consciousness. Other women claim that their memories and experiences as a birthmother do not intrude into their thoughts and lives very often, but when they do, the women feel surprised by the intensity of their reactions.

By the end of the first year, your life may appear as though it has returned to some semblance of normalcy. You may have returned to work or started a new career. You might have taken up where you left off in school, or begun a new school program. You most likely will be socializing and having fun with friends and family members. You may be dating or working on improving old relationships.

By this time, your relationship with the adoptive parents is probably more established, and you may be more comfortable with each other. Your adoption is probably finalized, although some adoptions take longer than a year. The adoptive parents are most likely more at ease since the adoption has been finalized in court. You are, hopefully, at peace with your adoption decision, although there may still be an ache in your heart for the child you placed for adoption.

The First Birthday

Even if you are happy with your decision and enjoy a satisfactory relationship with the adoptive parents, your baby's first birthday can be a difficult day. All the joy and sadness you experience that day may overcome you in a way you hadn't anticipated. The anniversary date of any loss is a time to revisit the feelings of that experience. You will find yourself thinking a lot about your baby during this period, and if you haven't had much contact with the adoptive family, you will wonder what your baby looks like and how he is doing. As birthmother counselors, we notice a heightened level of anxiety, depression, agitation, anger and self-destructive behavior in birthmoms as their yearly anniversary date approaches. Some women are perplexed about why their emotional health seems to be in a tailspin, until they are reminded that their birthchild's birthday is coming up.

Some adoptive families choose to include their birthmoms in the baby's birthday celebration. Even if you don't formally celebrate your child's actual first birthday with him and his family, there are many ways to mark the passage of the first year.

One adoptive family we know celebrates their child's adoption day (the day the adoption was finalized) with their child's birthparents. Another family celebrates the day they met their birthmother because they feel that is the day their child came into their life. Some adoptive parents and birthparents have a small, private party around the birthday. These kinds of get-togethers require a very open adoption. In cases where the adoption is less open or where the birthparents and adoptive parents live far from one another, birthmothers can still celebrate the first and subsequent birthdays in a more personal fashion. We definitely recommend some kind of a recognition or affirmation of the adoption, your role as a birthmother and your child.

This could be a time for quiet reflection, prayer or meditation or some private outing to symbolize your child's first birthday, and your role in his life.

Maintaining an Ongoing Relationship

"I have a continually growing relationship with my son and his family. I get to visit him a couple of times a year, which is wonderful. His mother is incredible. She sends me, as well as members of my family, all sorts of wonderful things: pictures, letters, videotapes of the kids. She is a very thoughtful and loving person. I have the utmost love and respect for them all."

Many adoptive parents tell us they are saddened by birthparents that discontinue contact. These same adoptive parents may have been very reluctant or even scared to have an open adoption, but as they grow to love and care about the birthparents, and are educated in the importance of openness for the child, they are motivated to stay in touch.

"It's funny how initially I feared contact with my birthparent and now I treasure it. My daughter knows she is loved by her birthmom not because I have told her so but because she has been told this directly from her birthmom. This means the world to me as I know this contributes to my efforts to try to help her become a strong, well-adjusted young woman."

Some birthparents we have worked with chose to have very little or no contact with the adoptive family for the first few years. There is no right or wrong level of contact in an adoption, although the situation becomes much more complicated to incorporate openness, when an open adoption is not originally designed. Hopefully the people in your life will respect and support your own preferences regarding the relationship you have with your birthchild and the adoptive parents. If you do choose to have contact, however, it is important to keep your birthchild's needs and feelings in mind. If you send a card or a gift, or telephone every birthday and holiday season, for example, your birthchild will grow to expect and look forward to this special ritual and may be very disappointed if you decide not to continue the practice. Keeping the relationship up and the communication open in a consistent fashion is very important for your child's sense of continuity.

Life throws us curves, of course, and your future may include periods of time when your circumstances are chaotic. You might be moving frequently, or breaking up with a partner, or suffering from an illness. You might want to take a break from many of your relationships and focus your energy and time on getting settled or healed. If your birthchild and adoptive family are accustomed to hearing from you, it can be upsetting for them if you drop out of sight. A phone call or a note, briefly explaining your circumstances and your need to lay low for awhile, can assuage their worry. Reassurance that you will again reconnect when you are able is respectful and loving.

What if the adoptive parents cut off contact at some point in the adoption? Unfortunately, this happens, and there is no legal recourse for birthparents, although some states have passed legislation that requires a "post-adoption contact agreement" with the final adoption papers. The nature of the open adoption should be discussed and agreed upon with an adoption counselor present and then put in writing with copies for all parties. Too often, birthparents and adoptive parents have difficulty expressing their preferences honestly, and promises may be made that are difficult to keep over the years.

It is important for adoptive parents and birthparents to acknowledge to themselves and to each other that agreements regarding contact are most helpful when they are flexible over time and across differing circumstances.

"I am thankful every day when I think about how lucky my son is to have them as parents. I think I gave him the best gift a mother could give."

Your Personal Life

Your personal life will continue to ebb and flow over the years following the adoption. Your relationship with your own family and the birthfather will most likely change. You may notice that you are viewing the world through different eyes after the adoption. It is a very maturing and sobering experience, one that most of your friends and acquaintances won't truly understand.

Your friends and family members may tell you that you are dwelling on the adoption too much when you talk about your birthchild or the adoptive parents, especially after the first year of the placement. You may hear from people that it is time to "move on" or "snap out of it." Seeking out support groups, where you can talk to other birthparents that will listen to and understand your feelings, may be helpful, even after the first year of the placement. We have worked with birthparents who periodically "check in" with a support group, years after their placement. For example, here in the San Francisco Bay Area, there are several post-adoption organizations that provide birthparent education, counseling and support groups. You can look in the Yellow Pages or on the internet to find services in your geographical area.

> *"To see her with them makes me sad at times, but I see their faces, and I smile through the pain. I just wish I could have kept her and raised her, but there are so many reasons why I couldn't. My boyfriend and I try to take one day at a time and concentrate on our goals so that, when the time comes, we will be prepared to have a family."*

Dating and New Relationships
(Or, It's All Right to Have a Love Life after Adoption)

Because the adoption experience is very intense, many birthmothers spend so much time preparing for this momentous event that their other emotional needs are put on the back burner. Some say the relinquishment experience has brought them closer to the birthfather, but for others, the relationship with the birthfather has ended. Some birthmoms find it difficult to start new relationships because they are feeling raw and don't want to go through another loss if the relationship doesn't work out. Some worry that a new boyfriend won't understand or accept their adoption decision, and they are concerned about introducing a new partner into the adoptive family's life. Others rush into a new relationship because they want to make the sad feelings go away.

Meeting new people or dating can be a positive and healthy experience for you. You don't need to find the perfect partner or your "soulmate," but you might be able to have fun and enjoy life a little more fully. Yes, it probably will be scary. Recognize that you will be vulnerable and be careful not to expect a new love relationship to heal the hurt of your loss. But when you feel ready, you owe it yourself to rejoin friends and have some fun. Test the water as you get to know someone and trust yourself about when it is the right time to share your private matters, including your adoption story. You don't have to tell your date about the adoption the first time you go out together. Take things slowly and disclose your experience with adoption when you feel ready and safe.

Pregnant Again?

We have occasionally worked with birthparents who become pregnant again relatively soon after their adoption placement. Some birthparents are consciously choosing another pregnancy because they decide they are now ready to parent. For others, however, unconscious motivations are at work. You may be trying to replace the child you have lost. You may be craving the attention you received or the closeness you felt with the adoptive parents. You may feel that without being pregnant, your life has no purpose. Before entering into another sexual relationship, give some thought as to what your underlying desires and motivations might be. As much as you may wish to do so, you can't repeat the experience or replace the child you have placed for adoption. If you find yourself taking sexual risks, find yourself someone you can confide in and whose advice you trust.

Change in the Adoptive Family

Just as you find your life changing and growing as the years go by, so will the adoptive family's life. Some changes may be subtle and not affect you and your relationship with them at all, but other changes will be major. Many adoptive families decide to adopt a second child, often within two to three years after their first adoption. Not only will this bring another child into their lives, but also it will bring a new set of birthparents. You may be happy for the adoptive parents and at the same time feel unsettled and jealous, wondering if their relationship with new birthparents will alter their relationship with you. Talking to the adoptive parents about your fears is a good idea. They probably also worry about having another set of birthparents in their lives and wonder how it will impact their relationship with you. Sometimes adoptive parents ask the first birthparents to talk to the "new" birthparents because, after all, who could give them a better recommendation?

Some parents have gotten pregnant after adopting their first child. Invariably, the birthparents wonder if the adoptive parents will love their biological child more than their adopted child. In our experience, adoptive parents love their children equally and don't favor one child over the other, although they may love different things about different children, as all parents do.

Another change that may affect your relationship with the adoptive parents is moving to a new location. Since we live in a mobile society, chances are that either you or the adoptive parents will move once or more during your lifetimes. You may start your relationship living twenty miles from the adoptive parents, and five years down the line you may live two thousand miles apart. Although you may not be able to see each other as frequently, your relationship can endure and grow if everyone makes an effort to keep in touch.

Change Due to Divorce or Death in the Adoptive Family

Divorce or separation can be an unexpected and upsetting experience for the adoptive parents and for you. If you are like the majority of birthparents, you probably chose the adoptive parents because you wanted your birthchild to grow up in a two-parent family. Adoptive parents are not immune to the pressures and difficulties of maintaining a relationship and may decide to separate or divorce. Hopefully, if this does happen to your adoptive family, you will be able to maintain a relationship with both the mother and father. We suggest that before the adoption is finalized, adoptive parents and birthparents commit to each other to stay connected, for the sake of the child, no matter what. In the case of divorce or illness, the adoptive parents should apprise family members about their commitment to openness over time, and solicit their support.

Another extremely difficult experience is a long-term or debilitating illness or death of an adoptive parent. While this is relatively rare, it does happen, and the loss for you and for your birthchild will be a big one. The surviving parent will need your support and love during this difficult time.

Adoption through the Years

During your birthchild's life, the level of contact may change many times. Your birthchild may want more or less contact with you during different periods of his life. It is important that both you and the adoptive parents maintain a tone of flexibility, always deferring to what is important for the child at any given time. Younger children are more firmly attached to their parents, but as they grow older, they may decide to develop more independent relationships with friends and relatives. Most teens go through conflict with their parents and often do or say things to hurt them. This is perfectly normal and it's the only way they can truly separate. An adopted teenager might say, "I hate you. I'm going to live with my real parents." Or she may complain about how unfair her parents' rules are. Keeping open communication and a united front with the adoptive parents during this time is important. Offering support and understanding to your birthchild, without undermining the adoptive parents, is an important role you can play in your birthchild's development. Being there for your birthchild during this time, so you can talk openly and honestly about your reasons for choosing adoption, can enhance your birthchild's self-esteem and confidence. Unlike adult adoptees and birthparents that have a closed adoption, your relationship will not be based on fantasy and longing but on honesty and respect.

One thing that you can do to benefit your child is to do your part to foster a relationship with the adoptive parents characterized by respect and integrity. Adoptive parents, are human beings with fears, insecurities and vulnerabilities. Respecting their role, devotion and authority with your child will go a long way towards creating a mutually reciprocal relationship.

To end this chapter, we would like to reiterate that placing a child for adoption will forever affect your life, and who you become will be deeply colored by this choice. Once this particular path is chosen, it cannot be undone. On the other hand, acceptance can be achieved, and your experience as a birthmom can be incorporated into who you are and who you are yet to be.

"The adoption was the best thing that ever happened to me. There isn't a day that goes by that I don't think about my son and how happy he is. It makes me feel happy and confident."

Chapter 10:
THE OTHER IMPORTANT PEOPLE:
BIRTHFATHERS AND
FAMILY MEMBERS

Birthfathers

Although this book was written primarily for birthmothers, we wanted to devote a small section to issues that are particular to you—the birthfather.

Over thirty years ago, the American family began to drastically change shape at a pace never before experienced in our culture. Coinciding with the feminist and civil rights movements, mothers were returning to work, parents were divorcing and remarrying, and single men and women were choosing to parent alone at a rate unprecedented in our history. The word "family" has come to include many different combinations, and our schools and cultures reflect these changes. As women have become more represented in the work force, men have become more active as parents. Although change may seem slow in coming and stereotypes continue to abound, there is more and more acceptance and encouragement for men who want to participate more fully in their children's lives.

This trend is true in the realm of adoption as well. Until recently, birthfathers were not routinely involved in the adoption planning. Legal processes were initiated in order to terminate the birthfather's rights, but rarely was he involved in things like picking the parents, supporting the birthmom, or witnessing the birth. Adoptive parents, birthmothers, and professionals alike assumed that birthfathers were really not interested. Recently, however, literature, the media, and legislation have all begun to reflect the important position the birthfathers can play in their child's adoption. Whether or not they are still involved with the birthmom, fathers are being offered the opportunity to be involved in the adoption plan to whatever extent feels most comfortable. Again, change does not happen overnight, and birthmothers are still the primary focus in many respects, but adopted children today stand a much greater chance of knowing both their birthmother *and* their birthfather.

Your Legal Rights

The topic of a birthfather's legal rights is a complicated one and is outside the scope and expertise of this book. However, you can certainly get answers to any legal questions regarding your rights and the adoption by consulting an attorney. Adoption attorneys are well-versed in birthfathers' rights and are often willing to answer a few questions by phone. If you cannot afford to meet with an attorney, Legal Aid provides low-cost or free legal help in some communities and is located in the phone book under the governmental headings. Adoption agencies are good resources and can also answer adoption-related questions over the phone. State laws vary tremendously concerning adoption, and are constantly changing, so it is important for you to know your own state's adoption laws. The adoption branch of the State Department of Social Services is available to answer questions for you.

Your Role

Birthfathers can be husbands, boyfriends, acquaintances, and even "one-night-stands." You may find out about the pregnancy and the child when the birthmother does, at any point during the pregnancy, once the baby has been born, or after the child is placed in his adoptive home. You may find out directly from the birthmother, or from a less direct source like friends, family, or even by receiving legal papers alerting you of the impending adoption. While the birthmother's connection with the baby is very concrete and obvious (she is the one that is pregnant, after all), your involvement may be more vague. You may be unclear on what your role is, or how you would like to be involved. Many men in this position feel very out of control. Depending on your relationship with the birthmom, you may not have any notion of what will happen next.

When birthfathers first find out about the pregnancy, their initial reaction typically includes numbness and shock; disbelief in the form of denying that the child could actually be theirs; anger towards the birthmom, themselves, or the universe; and overwhelming terror of what will happen next. Your acknowledgement of the reality of the situation may happen in stages. First is accepting the untimely pregnancy. Next is facing the decision of whether to abort, parent, or choose adoption. Finally it is getting used to the idea of adoption, if that is the choice, and facing your own stereotypes of what adoption means to you. You and the birthmom may disagree about what the outcome of the pregnancy should be. This is one of those situations when meeting with a neutral party, such as a therapist, minister, or family friend, would be very helpful. Hopefully, you and the birthmother will be able to come to an agreement.

Despite the fact that you are more likely to be involved in the adoption proceedings than birthfathers in the past, you may need to be proactive in the process to assert your needs and desires. Adoption professionals are devoted to drawing birthmothers out, and focus on making sure that their needs are being attended to. Reaching out to birthfathers may not be much of a priority most likely probably because of stereotypes that birthfathers do not want to be involved.

Deciding on Adoption

It is very typical for birthfathers to initially disagree with the birthmother's desire to proceed with an adoption plan. This resistance can be for a number of reasons. Some men really do not understand or accept adoption. They may deeply love their child and feel compelled to take on the role and responsibility of parenting at this time. They may be strongly influenced by friends and family about what is "the right thing to do." Some men hope that a child might solidify or heal a relationship that is shaky. Or they might believe that parenting their child is the consequence that they must live with for their part in the "mistake." In addition to all of these objections to adoption, however, are situations when birthfathers resist the adoption solely because they are excluded and disrespected. When men threaten to disrupt or fight the adoption plan, they begin to be perceived as hostile by the birthmother, the adoption professionals and the prospective adoptive parents.

The most difficult part about whether or not to consent to the adoption is that many times, you have to make a pretty quick decision. Once the shock of facing an untimely pregnancy fades, it makes sense to focus your attention on whether you can be supportive of the birthmom's decision. You owe it to yourself and your child to explore your thoughts, feelings and life circumstances with someone who will not try to unduly influence you. An adoption attorney can answer your legal concerns. An adoption agency, facilitator or counselor can help you explore your ambivalence and examine the pros and cons. If you are in a relationship with the birthmom, and even if you are not, let her know that you need some time to sort out all your thoughts about the situation. Hopefully, it will soon become clear whether or not you are able to support an adoption plan and to what extent you want to be involved, during the pregnancy and afterwards. After you have made your decision, consult with your attorney and/or adoption facilitator about your next step.

If You Would Rather Remain Anonymous....

Some birthfathers will support the birthmom's decision to place their child for adoption, by signing the consent for adoption papers or the relinquishment papers (different state laws and different definitions of "father" apply here, determining what document you will be asked to sign), but will prefer no involvement in the adoption process. Others will avoid being identified at all and will refuse to sign the adoption consents. This will require the attorney for the adoptive parents to go to court, after the birth of the baby, to have the birthfather's legal parenting rights terminated. As we have mentioned, it would be a good idea to look over carefully any papers that are delivered to you or consult with an adoption professional to help you understand the implications of signing or not signing. One of the arguments for being active in the consent/relinquishment process is because of the impact on the child. As the child grows up and learns about her birthparents and her adoption, it can be reassuring for her to know that her birthfather participated forthrightly. If her parents have nothing to tell her about her birthfather, because he denied paternity or because he disappeared, the child might personalize the information and feel badly about herself. On the other hand, if you actively sign the papers and fill out the health history forms, your child will have concrete proof that you cared enough to provide for her a full complement of personal information.

As the Pregnancy Progresses

Assuming an adoption decision has been made, your level of involvement through the pregnancy and after the child is born is for you to discuss with the birthmother and adoptive parents. You may choose more limited involvement or want to fully participate. You may even feel unclear about what kind of involvement suits you. Some birthfathers work together with the birthmothers all along the way. They help the birthmom pick out the family, attend meetings and get-togethers, go to doctor appointments and attend the hospital tour. They might choose to be present at the baby's birth and discuss ongoing contact with the adoptive parents. Other birthfathers want much less involvement, agreeing to sign the birthfather consent papers, providing medical information for the adoptive parents, but not being actively involved in the adoption plans. Your participation may be limited by the birthmother if she is keeping you out of the loop. As it has been stressed earlier, an adoption facilitator can help clarify your expectations, navigate difficult and emotional decisions, and make plans for the future that all can agree on.

Even if you are involved in the pregnancy, the reality of the baby may take a while to sink in. Unlike the birthmother, you do not have concrete daily reminders of the pregnancy: morning sickness, medical appointments, feeling the baby kicking and growing bigger and bigger. There are emotional reminders for the birthmom that you may be protected from as well. As the pregnancy progresses, people you know, and even ones you don't, will comment, asking her whether she knows the gender, what she has named the baby and so forth. Because you are one step removed from the baby, it may be difficult to imagine or prepare for what it will feel like when she actually arrives.

Some birthfathers begin to have intense feelings right away. Guilt, remorse, sadness, loss, and disappointment begin during the pregnancy. Men sometimes feel they are "shirking their responsibilities" by not choosing to parent the baby. They fear the child will grow up resenting the decision and feel angry at the birthfather for not trying harder to make it work.

> *"My father left my mother and me when I was only two. He just left one day, never looking back, never contacting us again. It has been so painful not knowing. Was it something about me? Whenever I think about my own son, Evan, I wonder, 'How can I do the same thing? How can I leave Evan like that?'"*

Open adoption helps your birthchild understand why you placed him for adoption. You will have an opportunity to explain your dilemma to the child directly by writing a letter or staying in touch. This gives you the chance to let him know that your adoption decision was made because of circumstances in your life at the time, not because the child was in some way unlovable. As a matter of fact, you may try to express how very much you do love your baby. Also, if the adoptive parents are able to meet you and get to know you, they will be in a much better position to represent you well to your birthchild over the years and answer the child's questions honestly and lovingly.

Thinking about what is best for you, your child, and the birthmother is not selfish. In some cultures, communities, or religions, having children can be viewed as being successful or powerful. You may experience a lot of peer or family pressure to "face your responsibilities" or "keep the blood in the family." Just remember that the decision to parent has to fit *you* one hundred percent, not your community. The adoption choice is definitely not the easy way out of an untimely pregnancy, and it is in no way avoiding responsibility. In some ways, going through the adoption process is the most difficult option of all.

The Birth of the Baby

We have seen birthfathers time and time again become surprisingly emotional at the hospital after their child was born. As we mentioned before, you have been somewhat insulated from the emotional ups and downs of the anticipated adoption. You may have been feeling strong and solid during the pregnancy, but don't be surprised if you feel very out of control emotionally once the baby is actually born. Anticipate an onslaught of feelings and thoughts that have not surfaced thus far. Be sure that you, as well as the birthmother, have close supportive people to talk with during this most difficult time. As a birthfather, you are an essential part of your child's adoption. You can be a very important support person for the birthmother. You can be reassuring and provide very critical information for the adoptive parents. And for the adopted child, your birthchild, you can communicate either directly or indirectly, that she is loved and valuable.

Birthfamilies

"My family didn't want me to place my baby for adoption at first. They thought I'd regret it."

"They were very supportive of my decision throughout my pregnancy."

"I never told anyone in my family about the pregnancy or the adoption. They wouldn't understand. They would find a way to criticize me about the whole thing."

Placing a child for adoption impacts other members of the extended birthfamily in various ways and in differing degrees. Over the years, we have counseled many birth grandparents or members of the extended family whose children, brothers, sisters, nieces, or nephews placed a baby for adoption. Some family members were aware of and involved in the pregnancy and adoption plan, while others didn't know until after the birth. We have heard from grandparents who only learned years after the adoption that their grandchild was placed in an adoptive home. If you are the family member of a birthparent, you will experience many feelings about the adoption.

Birth Grandparents

For parents whose child is considering an adoption, your

involvement will depend on the relationship you have with your child. Your child may want support for her decision, but not ironclad, inflexible opinions. In most states, birthmothers, regardless of their age, do not need parental consent to place their baby for adoption. Your role in the adoption plan may be removed and unclear. As much as you may want to have input, your child needs your unconditional support during this time.

The losses for birth grandparents are many and complex. You may feel sadness at losing a grandchild, especially if your child chooses a closed adoption. You might also feel helpless because the choices your child faces are so profound. You may feel particularly angry and out of control. Or you could be proud of your child's ability to make a mature and thoughtful decision, whatever that decision is. Many young people who are faced with an unplanned pregnancy are also separating from their family. They need to experience independence in their lives and in their choices. There are many reasons why children don't tell their parents about their pregnancy and adoption plan:

- Fear. She may not know how you will react and expect a lot of anger.
- Shame. If your family doesn't talk about sexuality, choices, and birth control, your child may be ashamed to admit she is pregnant.
- Trauma. The pregnancy may be a result of incest or rape.
- Ignorance. Many birthparents don't realize they are pregnant until late in their pregnancy.
- Independence. Your child may want to do this on her own and worries that if she confides in you, you may try to sway her decision.

"Neither my parents nor my family knew I was pregnant. They found out the day she was born. They were in shock."

Tips for Birth Grandparents

If you discover your child is pregnant, there are some things you can do to make this incredibly difficult time a little bit easier for her and protect the quality of your relationship with her:

- First and foremost—listen.
- Explore all of the options with your child. Offer to help find a qualified counselor.
- State your point of view and support your child in theirs.
- Give input when asked.
- Let your child make her own decisions about the pregnancy and delivery.
- Don't interfere with your child's relationship with the adoptive parents.
- Don't bad-mouth the birthfather.
- See a counselor if you need help coping with your child's decision.
- Try to find a "support" birth grandparent, someone who has been through this already.
- Be kind to yourself. This is hard for you, too!

"My family was very supportive, and I could always talk to them about anything."

"My family was torn between believing that I would actually do it and disbelief that I could be so 'cold.'"

Understanding and believing in adoption is a process. It takes a little getting used to and some education. If your child is contemplating participating in an open adoption, it will help you to get familiar with some of the current ideas about adoption. The Resource Guide at the end of this book lists many of the most important books and web sites on the subject. Libraries and bookstores include books on adoption in their parenting section. In addition, many adoption agencies provide counseling and support group services for birth grandparents as well.

Facing an untimely pregnancy and then deciding to relinquish that baby for adoption will be one of the most difficult crisis periods in your child's life. It is a time that he or she really needs your unconditional support. If you are not in agreement with your child's plan for adoption, and you cannot see yourself supporting her, you might be missing out on an important opportunity to connect with her on a deep and profound level.

Brothers, Sisters, and Other Relatives

"What is my relationship to this child?" We have heard this and other questions from the extended family members of the birthparents. We have always firmly believed that an emotional relationship exists among biological relatives, even though a legal relationship doesn't. However, it is very important to be sensitive to the birth and adoptive parents and respect the relationship they have developed. Some birthparents we have counseled chose not to have much contact with their birthchild, but they have encouraged their extended family's involvement. Some adoptive parents are very comfortable with these relationships, while others are not and prefer all contact to go directly through the birthparent. If, as an extended family member, you desire some contact, speak to the birthparents about this and try to understand and respect their decisions.

> *"Everyone was very supportive . . . I don't know that I ever gave anyone the space to question my decision. I was so comfortable with it myself that I don't think they had any other choice. What I didn't find out until after I had signed the adoption papers was that my family was ready to set up a nursery and help me raise my baby if I changed my mind. That they never let on really impressed me. Never once did anyone ever try to change or question my decision."*

Chapter 11:
CIRCUMSTANCES WHICH REQUIRE ADDITIONAL THOUGHT, PLANNING, AND COUNSELING

This book was written primarily for women considering placing a child for adoption at birth or shortly after. This last chapter will briefly address adoption situations that merit special consideration and further exploration. Placing a child you have been parenting, placing a second or third child for adoption, or choosing a family with a different racial background or a non-traditional family will add another layer of complexity to your adoption planning. In these cases, we strongly urge you to seek professionals who have a particular expertise in the area. There are, for example, adoption agencies that specialize in older child placements or transracial adoptions. We will provide some suggestions to assist you in finding the right practitioner for your situation.

Placing a Child You Have Been Parenting

Adoption agencies and attorneys do receive calls from women parenting babies or young children inquiring about adoption. Most of these calls do not actually result in an adoption placement but are the desperate inquiries of women who might feel at the end of their rope. There are programs available for stressed-out parents, especially in urban areas, which offer respite care. Respite care is temporary, short-term care for those parents who feel overwhelmed with parenting and desperately need a break. Sometimes just a few hours a day away from your child will give you the down time you need to enjoy some private time for yourself. Your county Social Service department would be able to point you in the direction of finding respite care.

If, however, your parenting experience is getting harder and harder and you cannot cope or care for your child adequately, you might consider adoption. Counseling is essential if you are considering adoption for a child you have been parenting. If you call an adoption practitioner, an agency, or an attorney, be sure you can receive as much counseling as you need. One session is not enough, and most reputable organizations will suggest several sessions before you even begin working on an adoption plan. While making the decision, take some time to consider the vast implications a placement decision would have on both you and your child. You can call the Social Service department in your community to see if you have the option of temporarily placing your child in a foster home to allow some time and space while you are considering your options. If you are considering foster care, make sure you know what paperwork you will be required to sign and what legal issues are involved. If you have any concerns, ask an attorney to review the arrangement with you.

If and when you determine that an adoption placement is in your child's best interest, finding a facilitator and a family is, of course, the next step. You should have a list of questions ready when you call an agency, adoption facilitator, or attorney.

SAMPLE QUESTIONS IN OLDER CHILD PLACEMENTS

- Do you do infant placements? Older child placements?
- How many families do you have available to choose from?
- How much counseling can I receive before the placement?
- After the placement?
- Do you have foster care?
- How long after the placement do I have before I must sign a relinquishment or consent?
- Will I be able to visit my baby after he is placed with the adoptive parents?

- How will the transition of my child to the adoptive parents be handled?
- Will my child go immediately from my home to the adoptive parents' home?
- What can I do to prepare my child for the transition?
- How can I prepare my other children?

There are excellent books written to shed light on ways to help a child transition from one family to another, several of which are in our resource section. Most adoption professionals agree that the move of a child from one family to another ought to happen slowly. Perhaps you and your child can spend time with the adoptive parents in your home, in their home, and on other types of outings. Then perhaps a series of sleepovers that lengthen over time.

Although a slow transition may feel tremendously painful for you once you have made up your mind to place, children fare better when they are eased into a change of this magnitude. Your adoption professional can help you and the adoptive parents talk with your child through this process and guide you through this difficult and uncharted period.

Placing a Second or Third Baby for Adoption

If you are considering placing a second or third baby for adoption, there are emotional issues to think about before making an adoption plan. Your second adoption experience will be different than your first in many ways. It may be easier emotionally, or it may be more difficult. Some women go into a second adoption hoping to work out issues that didn't get resolved the first time. Chances are that your grief issues from your first adoption will resurface during this placement. We have worked with women who had very positive adoption experiences and yet couldn't go through a placement the second time, even though they thought their original loss issues were resolved.

If you are thinking about a second or third adoption, you will know more of what to expect logistically. You may make very different decisions than you did in the first adoption. You may decide on more or less openness, or you may decide on a different facilitator. If you are considering a second or third adoption, make sure you align yourself with someone who is sensitive to the additional complexities inherent in multiple grief experiences. Know that fully acknowledging the pain in letting go of one child might make placing another child for adoption too hard to bear.

- Do you want to use the same agency, attorney, or facilitator or choose someone new?
- Are you interested in the same adoptive parents? If so, do they know you are pregnant again? Would they consider another child?
- Would you like more contact? Less contact?
- If you are choosing different adoptive parents, do you want them to meet your first adoptive family, since the children will be siblings by birth?
- If you have children that you are parenting, have you thought about their reactions?
- Did you receive counseling in your first adoption, and if so, was it helpful?
- Do you think you might need additional counseling this time?
- Do you feel familiar with your own personal response to grief and loss?

Closed Adoption or No-Contact Placements

"I have no contact with the child. It would be too easy to want to ask for him back if I saw him face to face. The adoptive parents will be sending me pictures of him once a year."

"I was really never interested in knowing anything about who adopted my baby. At the time I became pregnant, I had two teenagers already. Dealing with them and their adolescence was about as much as I could handle at the time. Sabrina had just run away. I just couldn't handle another relationship."

Sometimes birthmoms opt to co-create a closed adoption because they are parenting another child and are fearful that they lack the skills to talk openly with their child. Difficult as it may be, your child needs for you to talk forthrightly about your adoption decision. Children deal much better with concrete information as opposed to thoughts and fears that they cannot confirm or disprove. Openness in adoption helps a young child's understanding. But if you decide on no contact, you can still help your child communicate their thoughts and emotions.

Another reason that we have heard about wanting to keep the adoption confidential is a birthparent being unsure that they will be able to handle all the emotions unleashed by placing their baby for adoption. Some birthmothers feel more safe and contained with confidentiality and privacy. They suspect that by keeping the adoption closed and their relationships tightly defined, they will be able to hold themselves together more easily. In addition, some birthmoms are anxious to put the pregnancy, the birth and the adoption behind them, and begin to create for themselves a more positive, optimistic future. They deliberately choose a closed adoption so that they can feel free to focus on personal changes.

After considering all your options and your personal circumstances, you may decide it will be easier to limit or have no contact with your child and the adoptive parents. It is your absolute right to choose the adoption that is right for you. It would be essential to find a family that can be flexible. In cases where the birthparents choose to have a fully closed adoption, adoptive parents are often saddened because they wanted to maintain a relationship after the placement. Contrary to popular belief, many adoptive parents want and even expect an open adoption and are disappointed if their birthparents choose not to keep in touch.

If you choose an adoption with no contact, we suggest you make allowances for the slight possibility that you might want to open up the adoption in the future. Ask your adoption counselor to inquire about how the adoptive parents feel about the possibility of openness in the future, and what steps you will need to take to reach out.

Transracial Adoptions

We use the term transracial adoption to describe any adoption where the ethnicity of the child and adoptive parents is dissimilar. Transracial adoptions can be successful if the birth and adoptive parents are conscious of the choices they are making and respectful of cultural differences. It is important to find a facilitator who has had experience with transracial placements and can guide you and the adoptive family through the pre- and post-adoption periods, someone who will be able to provide guidance throughout the years. Here are some questions for the agency or attorney you contact:

- What is your philosophy and experience with transracial adoptions?
- How do you prepare the adoptive parents for adopting transracially?
- How much counseling do you provide before and after the birth for me and for the adoptive family?
- Do you have a post-adoption program?
- How does the counseling you provide specifically address the cultural issues that may arise in this adoption?
- Do you have support groups for the adoptive parents? For the birthparents?

Choosing a Non-Traditional Family Placement

Adoption has traditionally been a very conservative and controlled institution. Most children were placed with two parents (married, of course), and there were few other options. Over the years, the field of adoption has opened up to include more "non-traditional" placements—transracial adoptions, placement with single moms and dads, and gay and lesbian parents. Although many agencies still only accept married couples as adoptive parents, it is possible to find many attorneys, agencies, and facilitators who have prospective adoptive parents who are single, gay, or lesbian. Most birthparents who choose non-traditional placements didn't set out looking for a single mother or a gay couple but were attracted to a letter or a profile that pictured and described the prospective parents. There are many reasons women choose these alternative placements, but mostly they look for people they think are going to be the very best parents for their child.

Single Parent Adoptions

Although one of the main reasons young women choose adoption is that they don't want to be a single mom, many birthmoms have had wonderful adoptions with single mothers and fathers. You may hear a lot of questions and comments like, "If you don't want to be a single mom, why are you placing your baby with one?" or "There are lots of nice married couples who want to adopt, in fact I have a friend . . ."

Single men or women can make really good adoptive parents, especially if you have a good connection and see eye to eye on the important issues. Again, it is important to ask good questions, such as, "How will your support system help you take care of your child?" "If you need to return to work, how will you juggle your work and family life?" "What arrangements are you planning to make in regards to childcare?" "How does your family and friends feel about you adopting a baby?"

Gay and Lesbian Adoptions

Without a doubt, this is one of the hottest issues in adoption today. There are states, agencies, and communities that do not support the concept or practice of allowing gay and lesbian singles or partners to adopt. On the other hand, there are some agencies that promote and support these adoptions, and there are some wonderfully successful gay and lesbian adoptions.

In gay and lesbian adoptions, there are often legal issues to consider. In many states, two unrelated people cannot adopt a child through an agency. One parent may need to be the "adopting" parent, and the other parent may not be able to adopt the child. Some judges can grant an adoption to two unrelated partners, even if the agency can't make a recommendation for approval. Recently, the American Academy of Pediatrics announced its support for gays and lesbians adopting their partner's children. A committee of the Academy issued a statement after a review of two decades of studies saying, "Most (studies) found that the children of gay or lesbian parents were as well adjusted socially and psychologically as the children of heterosexual parents." The Academy said, "legalizing second parent adoptions is in the best interest of the children because it guarantees the same rights and protections to homosexual families that are routinely accorded to heterosexual parents and their children." ("Group Backs Gays who Seek to Adopt a Partner's Child," Erica Goode, *New York Times*, February 4, 2002). If you are considering this type of adoption, it is very important to find a good attorney who knows the laws in your state regarding single parent or unmarried parent adoptions to sort through any legal requirements.

Another important factor to a successful gay or lesbian adoption is finding a sensitive adoption counselor who can support your choice and work with you and the adoptive parents throughout the process. The counselor can help you with issues relating to your family and talking to your child in the future. If the birthfather is involved, it is very critical for the adoption to have his support or consent if you choose gay or lesbian adoptive parents. He could oppose the adoption and put a halt to your plans if not in agreement.

Changing Your Mind after the Placement

"I knew the adoption wasn't right for me after I had Alex and he went home with his family. I couldn't go on with my life . . . I got Alex back after one month, but through the whole month, it never got any easier."

Although most women who make an adoption plan follow through with their original intent, there are women who cannot, and they ask for their baby back after the placement. The reasons these women change their mind about the placement are as varied as the women themselves, but there is usually a common theme: "I didn't know it would be this hard."

Changing your mind after the placement will be difficult for you and devastating for the adoptive parents, to say nothing of the disruption for the child. It is something to examine fully when making your original plan. We always ask women before the birth, "What would cause you to change your mind about your adoption placement?" and we usually hear, "Oh, I could never do that! This is what I want. I would never do that to Joe and Mary!" We are firmly convinced that most birthmothers do not change their minds to hurt the adoptive parents, but they just were not prepared for the intense emotional feelings and the grief that follows a placement.

The most common time a birthmother changes her mind about adoption is in the hospital and during the first month after the birth. A much smaller percentage of birthmothers, however, decide they want their child back several months later, or even up to a year after the placement, assuming their rights have not yet been terminated.

Another contributing factor to birthmothers changing their minds is a deteriorating relationship with the adoptive parents. One birthmother who asked for her child back describes her situation:

> *"I picked the prospective adoptive parents from a selection of photo books that couples had put together for "clients" like myself. My first criteria were religion and nationality. Then I looked over the types of lifestyles and locations. The first couple I chose decided to back out because they were afraid. The second couple seemed acceptable at first, but I soon found them to be 'fakes'—nothing like their book portrayed. Before the birth, they put on a real artificial front with me. They would call me just about every day to make sure I was still going to give them my child. They bugged me to the point that I had to have my attorney stop them. They also started making my doctor appointments without my consent and showed up in my town to escort me to the hospital and tried to get information from my doctor about me."*

While there are typical feelings of jealousy and resentment toward the adoptive parents following a placement, if you find that you are angry all the time and unable to talk to the adoptive parents, you should call you counselor. Sometimes minor misunderstandings can blow out of proportion in the very sensitive post-placement time frame. A session to discuss hurt feelings is often helpful during this critical period. We have worked with birthmothers and adoptive families who have been able to resolve these conflicts and move ahead with their adoption plan. We have also been involved in adoptions where the birthparents decided that placement was not the right option and decided to parent their child. If your counselor is truly objective and sensitive to both you and the adoptive parents, she will be able to help you sort through the maze of your feelings and come to a decision that is right for you.

If you have already placed your baby with the adoptive parents but are pretty sure you want your baby back, you need to talk with someone immediately. Talk to your counselor about how you are feeling. Sometimes just voicing your feelings will help you recognize the grief and sorrow associated with your loss. It becomes difficult to distinguish thoughts and feelings from needing to make an actual plan during the postpartum period. Most birthparents go through a time when they think they might want their baby back, even if they don't tell anyone. Some birthmothers have told us that at this point it can be helpful to talk to the adoptive parents, or even to go and visit them and the baby.

> *"I just kept having dreams of my baby crying. I would wake up and think he was crying because he missed me, or because the couple did not love him as much as I did. I just thought about him night and day. I decided to go visit. I really thought that maybe I would be taking him home that day, but I didn't tell anyone. The visit was hard, but I just knew I couldn't take him back. It wasn't about my being afraid of hurting his adoptive parents, but I just realized that he was as happy with them as he would be with me. They loved him completely, and I could see him any time I wanted to. I was still sad but relieved to be out of such turmoil."*

If you reach a point where you have firmly and irrevocably decided to ask for your baby back, there are issues to consider:

- Who will tell the adoptive parents? You? Your counselor?
- When will the baby be returned to you and under what circumstances?
- What is the legal status of your adoption?
- Will your family be involved?
- Is the birthfather aware that you are going to parent your baby? Is he supportive?

As difficult as it may seem, in most cases it is best if you talk to the adoptive parents about your plans to parent your child. If you have been working with a counselor, the counselor can be the one to initially tell them what your plans are, but it can be incredibly healing if this call is followed by one from you.

When a baby is returned to the birthmother, we suggest a joint meeting between the birth and adoptive parents at a neutral location with one or two counselors and support people. These meetings can be very emotional and intense, but they are incredibly important for healing. The adoptive parents are always deeply sad and often angry.

They feel betrayed. You probably feel a tremendous amount of guilt and sadness, mixed with relief. You both need a facilitator so you can express how you are feeling without things getting out of control.

In preparing for this meeting, try to remember that while there is sure to be anger, you can help the adoptive parents with the emotional process of moving through their pain just by your willingness to be present for a part of it. This may facilitate their ability to go on and eventually find success adopting another baby.

If You Do Change Your Mind

- **Be truthful.** Be open and honest about your reasons for wanting to parent now.
- **Be compassionate.** The adoptive parents will need understanding and compassion as they give up a child they have loved as their own.
- **Apologize.** You do not have to apologize for your decision to take your baby back, but consider expressing your sorrow at causing them pain. Reassure them, if this is true, that your decision had nothing to do with them, that you could not have picked a better family, but that you simply could not live without parenting your own child.
- **Be thankful.** Thank them for being such great parents and for loving your baby.
- **Let them grieve.** Be willing to listen to them express their feelings about losing the baby that they thought would be theirs. A facilitator can provide safety and structure for this expression of feelings.

> *"I am sorry that I hurt this wonderful family, and I regret missing the first month of my son's life. The only good thing is that instead of being forced to raise my son, it feels that I've chosen to."*

Closing Comments

The journey from first discovering you are pregnant to placing your child for adoption can be a long and often arduous one, but one also filled with hope and joy. Although some women ultimately decide this is not the right path for them, most women who place their babies with adoptive parents are able to follow through with their decision with a sense of pride and accomplishment. Adoption is not an easy choice. It requires a mixture of determination, patience, the willingness to take risks, and vulnerability to emotions.

If adoption is your choice, we sincerely hope we have been able to provide you with some understanding, knowledge, and most importantly, some practical tools that you can use along the way. We hope you will find peace with your decision.

RESOURCE GUIDE

Books for Birthparents and their Families

Adoption: A Handful of Hope (originally published in 1983 as *To Love and Let Go*); Suzanne Arms, Celestial Arts, 1989; stories about women who have relinquished their babies for adoption (out of print).

The Adoption Reader: Birthmothers, Adoptive Mothers and Adopted Daughters Tell Their Stories; Susan Wadia-Ellis, Seal Press, 1995; 30 women talk about how adoption has affected their lives.

A Birthmother's Book of Memories; Brenda Romanchik, R-Squared Press, 1994; a fill-in-the-blanks book for a birthmother to describe her own family, friends, and life; can make a wonderful gift for a child.

Birthmother's Day Planner; Mary Jean Wolch-March, R-Squared Press, 1997; a useful tool to plan an event to honor a birthmother.

Birthmothers: Women Who Have Relinquished Babies for Adoption Tell Their Stories; Merry B. Jones, Chicago Review Press, 1993; stories about 70 women who have relinquished their babies.

Dear Birthmother, Thank You for Our Baby; Kathleen Silber and Phyllis Speedlin, Corona Publishing Co., San Antonio, 3rd edition, 1998; one of the classic books on open adoption, contains letters between birth and adoptive parents.

Fathers Failing and Healing: A Spiritual Meditation; (expanded version of *Dear Birthfather*); Randolph W. Severson. Ph.D., Heart Words Center, 1997; useful for fathers after placement or loss.

Life Givers: Framing the Birthparent Experience in Open Adoption; James Gritter, Child Welfare League of America, 2000; description of the birthparent experience from an adoption social worker.

My Child Is a Mother; Mary Stephenson, Corona Publishing, 1994; a personal account by a birthgrandmother of her daughter's experience (out of print).

Never Never Never Will She Stop Loving You; Jolene Durrant, Jobiz, Inc., 1999; a children's book tells the story of a birthmother and the child she placed for adoption.

The Other Mother: A Woman's Love for the Child She Gave up for Adoption; Carol Schaefer, Soho Press, 1991; a woman's personal story about her search and reunion with the son she placed for adoption.

Out of the Shadows: Birthfather Stories; Mary Martin Mason, O.J. Howard, 1995; interviews with fathers who are not parenting their children.

Pregnant? Adoption Is an Option: Making an Adoption Plan for a Child; Jeanne Warren Lindsay, Morning Glory Press, 1996; discusses planning as a key to making an adoption plan.

Reunion: A Year in Letters Between a Birthmother and the Daughter She Couldn't Keep; Katie Hern and Ellen McGarry Carlson, Seal Press, 1999; this book is a collection of letters written over a year's period between a birthmother and the daughter she placed for adoption.

Shattered Dreams, Lonely Choices: Birthparents of Babies With Disabilities Talk About Adoption; Joanne Finnegan, Bergin and Garvey, 1993; explores options for parents with special needs children.

What Is Open Adoption; Birthparent Grief; Being a Birthparent: Finding Our Place; Brenda Romanchik, R-Squared Press, 1999; booklets for birthparents.

Your Rights and Responsibilities: A Guide for Expectant Parents Considering Adoption; Brenda Romanchik, R-Squared Press, 1999; a guide booklet for prospective birthparents.

Books on Grief and Loss

Crossing the Bridge: Creating Ceremonies for Grieving and Healing From Life's Losses; Sydney B. Metrick, Celestial Arts, 1994; a self-help book for those who have experienced a loss.

The Grief Recovery Handbook: The Action Program for Moving Beyond Death, Divorce and Other Losses; John J. James, Russell Friedman, Harper Collins revised edition, 1998; step by step guide book for recovering from loss.

The Healing Sorrow Workbook: Rituals for Transforming Grief and Loss; Peg Elliott Mayo, New Harbinger Publications, 2001; a guide-book, including rituals for those in grief.

Helping Children Cope with Separation and Loss; Claudia Jewett Jar-ratt, Harvard Common Press, 1982; although primarily written for adoptive parents, this book discusses a child's reaction to loss.

How to Survive the Loss of a Love; Melba Colgrove, Harold H. Bloomfield, Peter McWilliams, Prelude Press, 1991; poems, stories, and words of wisdom for those who have experienced a loss.

Saying Good-bye to Baby, Volume 1: The Birthparent's Guide to Loss and Grief in Adoption; Patricia Roles, Child Welfare League, 1989; a book about loss and grieving in adoption for birthparents.

Saying Good-bye to Baby, Volume II: A Counselor's Guide to Loss and Grief in Adoption; Patricia Roles, MSW, Child Welfare League of America 1990; a good resource for counselors working with birthpar-ents.

Books on Pregnancy

The Pregnancy Journal: A Day-to-Day Guide to a Healthy and Happy Pregnancy; A. Christine Harris, Ph.D., Chronicle Books, August 1996; daily guidebook for pregnant women.

What to Expect When You Are Expecting; Arlene Eisenberg, Heidi

Murkoff and Sandee Hathaway, Workman Pub. 1991; a comprehensive guide to pregnancy.

Special Circumstances

If you are considering placing your child with a family of another ethnic background, a single parent, a disabled parent or a gay or lesbian parent, these books may offer additional insight.

Adopting on Your Own: The Complete Guide to Adoption for Single Parents; Lee Varon Farrar Strauss & Giroux, September 2000; a guidebook for single parents seeking to adopt.

A Handbook for Single Adoptive Parents; Hope Meredian, National Council for Single Adoptive Parents, 1992; a how-to guide for single adoptive parents filled with information and encouragement.

Inside Transracial Adoption; Gail Steinberg and Beth Hall, Pact Press, 2000; a thorough guide for all involved in transracial adoption.

In Their Own Voices: Transracial Adoptees Tell Their Stories; Rita James Simon and Rhonda Roorda, Columbia University Press, 2000; personal stories from African-American and bi-racial adoptees, adopted by Caucasian parents.

Issues in Gay and Lesbian Adoption; Ann Sullivan, editor, Child Welfare League of America, 1995; addresses questions and issues in gay and lesbian adoptions.

The Lesbian and Gay Parenting Handbook: Creating and Raising Our Families; April Martin, Harper Perennial, 1993; covers an array of topics including adoption.

Of Many Colors: Portraits of Multiracial Families; Peggy Gillespie, University of Massachusetts Press, 1997; stories and photos of American families who lived in multiracial families formed through adoption and marriage.

Transracial Adoption: Children and Parents Speak; Constance Pohl and Kathy Harris, Watts, 1992; explores the complex issue of transracial adoption through stories of families.

The Question of David; Denise Sherer Jacobson, Creative Arts Book Company, 1999; the true story of a couple with cerebral palsy who adopt a healthy baby.

General Books on Adoption

Adopting the Older Child; Claudia Jewett Jarratt; Harvard Common Press, 1978; describes the transition from the honeymoon period through the testing period to the integration of a child into a family.

Adoption Without Fear; James Gritter, Corona Publishing, 1989; first hand accounts of adoptive parent's experiences with open adoptions.

Children of Open Adoption; Kathleen Silber and Patricia Martinez Dorner, Corona Publishing, 1989; looks at the effects of open adoption on children from infancy through the teenage years, using a developmental approach.

The Family of Adoption; Joyce Maguire Pavao; Beacon Press, 1999; a well written resource for all involved in adoption.

Ghost at Heart's Edge: Stories and Poems on Adoption; Susan Ito, editor, Tina Crevin, Jacquelyn Mitchard, North Atlantic Books, 1999; short stories and poems about adoption from a variety of authors.

Open Adoption: A Caring Option; Jeanne Warren Lindsay, Morning Glory Press, 1987; presents open adoption from a highly positive view.

The Open Adoption Experience; Lois Melina and Sharon Kaplan Rosia, Harper Perennial, 1993; a guide to adoption for adoptive and birthfamilies.

The Spirit of Open Adoption; James Gritter, Child Welfare League of America, 1997; thorough presentation of open adoption.

Toddler Adoption – The Weavercraft; Mary Hopkins Best, Perspective Press, 1998; covers all aspects of adoption and parenting young children.

Other Resources

There are many resources on the Internet about all aspects of adoption. In addition to general information about adoption, there are sites set up especially for birthparents. Many agencies, attorneys and facilitators have web sites about their services. This is a good place to start gathering information and getting an idea of what type of organization will suit your needs. Additionally, many adoptive parents post their birthmother letters online. If you don't have access to a computer, most libraries have computers with Internet accessibility. Call your local library to see if this is an option for you. Some of the resources we have found to be helpful are:

National Adoption Information Clearinghouse
330 C St. SW
Washington, DC 20447
703-352-3488
888-251-0075
www.calib.com/naic/
An excellent resource for new and updated adoption issues

American Adoption Congress
P.O. Box 42730
Washington, DC 20015
202-483-3399
www.americanadoptioncongress.org
Services for all members of the triad

PACER
Post Adoption Center for Education and Research
P.O. Box 31146
Oakland, CA 94605
925-935-6622 or 888-746-0514
www.pacer-adoption.org
An excellent resource for information and support on all aspects of adoption.

Roots and Wings
P.O. Box 577
Hackettstown, NJ 07840
908-813-8252
www.adopt-usa.com/rootsandwings
Articles about all aspects of adoption.

PACT, An Adoption Alliance
3220 Blume Drive Suite 289
Richmond, CA 94806
510-243-9460
www.pactadopt.org
Publishes PACT Booksource, a comprehensive reference guide to
adoption books; also specializes in transracial adoption issues.

Tapestry Books
www.tapestrybooks.com
P.O. Box 359
Ringoes, NJ 08551
1-800-765-2367
An excellent resource for adoption books, including many listed
in this reference guide.

Insight
R-Squared Press
721 Hawthorne
Royal Oaks, MI 48076
810-543-0997
www.r2press.com
Adoption resources for birthparents.

Decision Making Grid (amended from _The Skills of Helping_;
Robert Carkhuff, 1979) Contact editor if you would like a copy of this
useful tool.

E-mail for Leslie Foge lfoge@aol.com

E-Mail for Gail Mosconi gmmosconi@yahoo.com

Visit us @ our website: www.thirdchoicebooks.com

Leslie Foge, MA, MFT, was born and raised in the San Francisco Bay Area, where she still lives and practices. She received her Bachelors Degree in Psychology from UC Berkeley, and her Masters Degree in counseling from St. Mary's College. Leslie sees children, adolescents, adults, couples, and families in her private psychotherapy practice in Northern California, where she specializes in working with triad members. She is a popular workshop and conference presenter and is on the faculty at St. Mary's College.

Gail Mosconi, MSW, LCSW, is a native Californian and Licensed Clinical Social Worker who has worked with children and families in many different settings for over 30 years. She received her Bachelors Degree in Sociology from UC Santa Barbara, and her Masters Degree in Social Work from Sacramento State University. Her social work career includes working with emotionally disturbed children and teens, children and adults with disabilities, mental health and adoptions. She currently lives in Northern California and works in the mental health field.